Ain't Nothin' But a Winner

Ain't Nothin' But a Winner

BEAR BRYANT, THE GOAL LINE STAND, AND A CHANCE OF A LIFETIME

BARRY KRAUSS and JOE M. MOORE

With a Foreword by Don Shula

The University of Alabama Press Tuscaloosa

The University of Alabama Press
Tuscaloosa, Alabama 35487-0380

Manufactured in the United States of America
Designer: Michele Quinn
Typeface: Minion and Frutiger

∞

The paper on which this book is printed meets the minimum
requirements of American National Standard for Information
Sciences-Permanence of Paper for Printed Library Materials, ANSI
Z39.48-1984.

Library of Congress Cataloging-in-Publication Data

Krauss, Barry.
    Ain't nothin' but a winner : Bear Bryant, the goal line stand, and a
chance of a lifetime / Barry Krauss and Joe M. Moore ; with a foreword by Don Shula.
        p. cm.
    ISBN-13: 978-0-8173-1541-2 (cloth : alk. paper)
    ISBN-10: 0-8173-1541-1 (alk. paper)
    1. Krauss, Barry. 2. Football players—United States—Biography.
3. Bryant, Paul W. 4. Football coaches—United States. 5. Indianapolis
Colts (Football team)—Biography. 6. Baltimore Colts (Football
team)—Biography. I. Moore, Joe M., 1956– II. Title.
    GV939.K735 2006
    796.332092—dc22
                                                        2006006856

CONTENTS

FOREWORD

Don Shula

Ain't Nothin' But a Winner: Bear Bryant, The Goal Line Stand, and a Chance of a Lifetime is about Barry Krauss's love of football. It is about football as a way of life and how Krauss's blessed journey through life included learning the game from one of its all-time best apostles, Paul W. "Bear" Bryant.

Today, hundreds, perhaps even thousands, of players and former players suffer the loss of football in their lives when they stop playing—a malady called separation anxiety. This happens to players of all levels, from peewee, to high school, college, and the pros. To almost every one of them, it happens before they would have chosen.

The first time I looked into Barry's eyes after he retired, I saw a peace there that only the purest of players can have. Barry always left every ounce of his being on the field; he held nothing back. Only this type of player can walk away from the game whole.

Barry Krauss is a whole man.

ACKNOWLEDGMENTS

Foremost, I would like to thank my father—my hero—for everything. He did it all, from throwing the baseball with me, to playing football, to teaching me about working on the car. He always did more than he had to, from carrying me over the hot sand at the beach, to fixing my bike, to staying up with me after one of those childhood nightmares.

Thank you to my mother. She was always at my games cheering for me, whether at Pompano, Alabama, the Colts or the Dolphins.

"Is that your mother yelling?" I can still remember my teammates asking. She has always been a full-throated supporter of Barry Krauss.

My mom prepared me to play in every way. She would even get up before the crack of dawn and create our own little special concoction—a growth potion that consisted of a half-gallon of milk, a half-gallon of ice cream, a dozen eggs, and chocolate flavoring. Thanks to her efforts, I went from 5′11″ and 185 pounds, to 6′3″ and 225 pounds the summer after my junior year.

Coach Bryant taught me that college was not only a place to learn something but a place to become somebody. He taught me how we can make a difference not only on the field but also in life. He prioritized life: faith, family (call your momma), and then football (Alabama).

Thank you Coach Shula for being an approachable hero, for giving me the opportunity of a lifetime, and for allowing me to fulfill my dream of playing for you and the Miami Dolphins.

To Bob, my big brother, I owe a special debt of gratitude. He taught me how to play linebacker and protected me as a skinny kid with a dream. I will always welcome being known as "Bob Krauss's little brother."

To my little brother Erik, my war hero, thanks for protecting our country and our freedom. I am very proud of you.

And to my soul mate and wife, Darcy, thank you for hanging with me through the tough moments in life. Your love at the lowest moment of my life made it all worthwhile. You are a wonderful woman who never needs makeup and is always beautiful. You loved me when I wasn't very lovable, gave me your opinions when I didn't want them (knowing you were right), and stayed with me in my constant, never-ending transition from football.

Best of all Darcy, you listened to all of my dreams and helped make them come true.

To Ashley, my oldest daughter, who is in New Zealand at this writing, I think about you and miss you every day. Ashley was raised crimson and white and could say "Roll Tide" and "Amabama" from the time she was born.

Thank you to my sweet and caring Charlsie, my charismatic and athletic Savannah, and my kind, loving son, Karsten, my "mini-me."

And to My Lord Jesus Christ, thank you for giving me purpose and passion for life. Thank you, Lord, for carrying me when I needed to be carried, teaching me the true fundamentals of life when I needed to be taught, and, most important, for trusting me to learn to let go and trust you.

Perhaps most important, thank you to my teammates who were on the field with me that day. Their input and cooperation helped make this project truly special.

And to Joe Moore, my partner, confidant, and close friend, thank you for always being there for me.

Barry Krauss

◆

There are some dramatically special moments in everyone's journey through life which shape their world to come. Someone really in-tune with people, fate, and the natural universe can see them coming. Many of us have to recognize them from our feelings.

When I met my wife, Carol, I got one of those life-changing feelings. More than anything, she believes in loving her family. She has taught me well.

I experienced three other dramatically special moments when I witnessed the births of Haley, Emily, and Burke—my children. They are wonderful people and a great support system. They are also powerful and inspiring forces to prove every day that there is a God and He is good. Because of them, I know I will have a tremendously positive impact on this world long after I am gone.

Thank you to my father, Joe Ray Moore, who taught me his work ethic. He also showed me how a father truly loves his children, through everything he does and says.

And thank you to Barry, who on a hot fall afternoon in 1975, jumped into a hole as I took a hand-off on a 40-trap and put me out of football. The true irony here is that, working together on this project, we have put each other "back into football."

Joe M. Moore

1

Chance of a Lifetime—It's All about Dreams

The world of sports in America *is* America.

For many like me, sports are all-encompassing. The love of competition is absorbed through our pores and soaked into our very being almost from birth. It courses through our veins and pours out our sweat glands. It is our being. And, to a select and lucky few, it forges us into people who can be involved in something fantastic, supernatural, and almost surreal—a great play that lives on throughout time, not just changing the outcome of a game but affecting the lives of participants and fans for years and decades to come.

There is a true irony here: the play is over in an instant, yet it lives on forever. We never lose our memory of it, and we can never walk away from its impact on our lives. And for those of us who are lucky enough to have ever been involved in one of those plays, we instantly know that we have experienced a "chance of a lifetime."

These things don't just happen as a natural occurrence in the universe.

Every "chance of a lifetime" starts with the dream—maybe one from early childhood—which even the dreamer is perhaps too bashful to admit. Then it turns into hard work, more dreaming, building a future, working even harder, and finally—if everything goes perfectly—the realization of that one chance to fulfill "the dream."

My dream as a third grader growing up in Pompano Beach, Florida, was to play for Don Shula and the Miami Dolphins. You know, the "Big Guy Upstairs" has a great sense of humor when giving us dreams. Sometimes our dreams are realized, sometimes not, but most of the time just striving to fulfill those dreams makes us better people. Great sense of humor, and He knows what He's doing. More about that dream and one of its true believers, my third-grade teacher, Mrs. Sayer, later.

Anyway, success is always elusive. On every athletic field and court, whenever there is a "chance of a lifetime," the outcome can fall either way. Each team has to reach out and grab it, squeeze it—hold it like the children we love so much today— for at that time in our life this "chance of a lifetime" *is* our life.

It would be pretentious to believe that my chance was any different, any more special, or had any more impact than anyone else's chance. They are all dramatic. They are all life-changing "significant emotional events."

It just so happens that my chance of a lifetime came about in football. Probably more important, it came about in the 1978 NCAA National Championship football game, Alabama vs. Penn State, in a Sugar Bowl game that was televised nationally on the afternoon of January 1, 1979. The whole world was watching.

Maybe equally important, I was on a team formed and forged by Paul W. "Bear" Bryant at the instant he won the fifth of his six national championships. He would win another the following year.

In true Bear Bryant form, he praised everyone but himself.

"As for me," he said, "and I'm sincere, I contribute so little that I take a lot of pride in being a part of something like this."

What a coach! What a man!

Coach Bryant knew the secret. In sports the chance of a lifetime seldom comes to those who are just talented, just well-coached, or just lucky. It comes—quite honestly—to those who are all of the above. And it only comes to a minuscule few of those.

When it does come—when you get that one chance of a lifetime to make your greatest of dreams come true—it changes everything.

And in the white-hot spotlight of sports in this nation—the impact is colossal.

It is this full understanding of how special, how rare, and how universally unique it is to capitalize on a chance of a lifetime, that my collaborator, Joe Moore, and I have created the Chance of a Lifetime book series, which tells the stories of athletes all over the world who realize their dreams, each through their own "chance of a lifetime."

This book will exhibit how my life evolved from that of a kid without much self-confidence to a young man molded and so inspired by Coach Bryant that I, we—the entire team—refused to give up. We will follow our team's ride, and my small part in it, to that historic moment in New Orleans.

This book also chronicles how my "chance of a lifetime" opened new doors for me personally and professionally in the NFL. It follows my career, my life, through its ups and downs toward today.

Perhaps most important, this book shows how the hard work, dedication, and focus of one man, Paul W. Bryant, shaped the lives of football players, men, students, fans, and the people of the state of Alabama for more than two generations.

2

Pompano, Football, and Life in a Pink House

Life in Pompano Beach, Florida, would seem to be somewhat idyllic. Beautiful views, the beach, peaceful . . . quiet.

Hardly. Not with Barry Krauss around.

Don't get me wrong; it wasn't *just* me. It was my entire group. Well, possibly it *was* me to a greater extent than my friends.

I can still remember approaching any number of friends' houses and seeing their mothers hurry to close their drapes when they saw me coming. I didn't take it personally. I just assumed that their front yard was closed for the day.

Oh, yeah, I forgot to mention that any lawn in Pompano was our potential football field. That could have been one of the problems. Most of the time it was the front yards—where there was really nice grass. When we were through with one lawn, it would have a completely worn-out middle, just like a real grass football field. Like a swarm of locusts, we would move on to another perfect lawn. And by the way, we used everything in the yard. Those exquisitely manicured shrubs, a perfect goal line. We dove over them to score. Over the top. Yea! Touchdown at any cost. And sprinkler heads, the ideal end-zone pylons—especially if they were up and sprinkling.

And all the havoc we created meant nothing to us. We were oblivious.

Eventually all the parents got wise, and we wound up either skateboarding or riding our bicycles to Kester Park, in Old Pompano, or just playing in the streets. Of course there was that pesky issue of cars. We were tough though. We would stop the game as they passed, but we'd let them know we didn't appreciate their interference. We'd smear our dirty hands down the side of the cars or yell something smart like, "Don't come back through here today!"

We were *so* tough.

Is it any wonder I was always running from someone? I had a mouth, a little talent, and was a little cocky. Sometimes the combination got me into trouble. Of course, being the only kid in the entire world to live in a pink house didn't help. Any of the bigger or older kids that wanted to make a statement would find me, the kid in the pink house, and beat me up. Looking back now, I realize that I never really got beat up—more like pushed around. But I was always in fear of being chased and caught. It seemed that someone was always running hard behind me. I sincerely believe that feeling is what shaped my personality, the personality that Coach Bryant immediately read and began to mold into a football player.

I loved football. I was so competitive that I didn't want to leave the field to get a drink—I would drink puddle water so I wouldn't miss anything. Sometimes, if I was around the house on Saturdays, my mom would put me to work. Make the bed. Vacuum the house. Clean the windows. Wash the cars. Cut the grass. It was endless.

Although I didn't know it at the time, Mom and Dad were teaching me some great habits and, as I learned much later, wonderful lessons. This was an area in which Dad excelled: he taught lessons by example, not by preaching at us. In fact, my dad always preferred showing leadership to talking leadership. Perhaps this was where I learned one of my most important lessons.

As a rambunctious eight-year-old, I was pretty rough on everything, particularly my bicycle. It was my lifeline, my instant travel machine, my ticket to neighborhood football games all across Pompano.

You must remember that those were much more innocent days than the ones we live in now. A child with a bicycle had almost limitless possibilities. There were no boundaries.

I used my bike . . . really used it. However, I was not very prone to care for it as well as I should. One Saturday morning I built up my courage and approached Dad in his garage workshop. I rolled in my dilapidated bicycle—which was probably less than a year old.

"Look, Dad," I'm sure I started out convincingly. "This thing is really beat-up, and a lot of the kids have new bikes."

Dad looked around the garage as if to check on the new bike inventory. He glanced at his watch as a huge grin came over his face.

"OK," he said, "let's get you a new bike."

He went straight to his toolbox and began handing me tools and orders. "First take off the handlebars."

As an eight-year-old boy can sometimes rationalize, I figured, "Great, we're going to take this thing apart before we go to the store for the new one." Soon we had parts strewn throughout the garage. We were sanding pieces here and oiling parts there. All of a sudden it was kind of fun. And then it was afternoon.

After lunch we got into the car and drove to the hardware store. We walked right by the row of new bikes, only to stop at the spray paint display.

"What color do you want your new bike to be?" he asked.

All of a sudden, I thought I got it. We were going to just fix my bike. I was so disappointed.

Trying to be difficult, I told him I wanted it red . . . metallic red, with racing stripes . . . and numbers . . . and other decorations. When we walked out we had all the paint we needed, I needed, to do the job.

Back at the garage we took great care in painting the frame and then painstakingly reassembled the bicycle. By the time that was done, the frame was dry enough to add the racing stripes. Just as Dad and I finished those, Mom called us in to dinner. It was almost dark.

The next day, the kids in the neighborhood were all enthralled by my "new," customized, bike. I accepted their compliments, never letting on that we had done it ourselves.

It was only years later that I realized exactly what had happened that day. Dad could have easily bought me a new bike and got on with whatever he was doing that morning, but instead he wanted to teach me, firsthand, the values of work and caring for my property. Much more important, he spent time with me. He was teaching me about fatherhood and the value of that relationship.

As a rambunctious eight-year-old, though, I didn't see it. At that age the lesson it reinforced was, "Once you get out of the house on Saturday, don't go back."

So, from that day on, once I was out of the house and had a game going, I never went back until I was on the edge of death.

A POWERFUL WILL TO WIN, OR A HORRIBLE TEMPER

As a child I was told repeatedly about how I must somehow overcome my temper. For me it was not a temper issue—it was an enormous will to win. With God as my witness today, I say there is a difference, and I know it. Still, that doesn't change my childhood.

Nothing ever hit me harder than one event in my sixth-grade year. A tradition at our elementary school demanded that the sixth graders play the faculty in a softball game toward the end of the school year. The faculty had watched me play all year: they knew my drive to win, as well as the resulting blowups when I did not. Prior to the game it was announced that, because of my temper, I would not be allowed to participate in that year's traditional game. What an embarrassment; in front of the whole school, I had to sit out of this game! I had never been so brokenhearted. Looking back, I'm sure I deserved it, but it still hurts.

First "Organized" Football

Little League Football on the South Pompano team was a hoot. I was such a wimp. I hated practice but loved the games. Wait, maybe not a wimp but a quarterback. Yeah, that's what I was. Now I remember, I was a quarterback/running back.

My days on offense were hard. Thankfully, they ended abruptly. While playing QB, I called a sweep right and forgot the play at the line of scrimmage. Yep, you're getting ahead of me. I, the quarterback, ran the wrong way. The whole backfield went right with the sweep and I went left. The cornerback, Clarence Jones, grabbed me and slung me to the ground, breaking my arm. I remember the pain—to this day, I remember it as some of the most horrendous I ever had in football. Of course, my coach checked it out and said I just pulled a muscle. I sat out the rest of the day and rode my bike home, about five miles. My arm hurt so bad I just cried all the way home. My dad helped me into the shower and took me to the hospital for x-rays.

That day I pledged that I would never let anyone do that to me again. It was that very day that I evolved—changed in every way—to defense. I could be the hitter. I could inflict the pain on other kids. Yeah.

Baseball—My Second Love

Ironically, the thing I liked most about baseball was the contact. The contact—can you believe that? I was a catcher. I controlled the game, called the pitches, worked the psychology, played the umpire, and knew every player on the opposing teams, so I could place our defense. But what I lived for and loved most was seeing a runner turn third base with a full head of steam and knowing I was going to get to really smash the guy.

I also loved to throw runners out on the base paths. I dared them to steal. I threw at them on first base as they got a lead. I would throw *at* them on second and on third. I wanted them to know I wanted their heads. I wanted to intimidate them.

One time, another catcher and a friend of mine, George Sammons, was up at the plate. I nicknamed him "Hotdog" because he was arrogant and cocky. We used to talk tough to each other because we were both so competitive. We battled constantly to be known as the best catcher in the league. (By the way, I played for a great sponsor: Southern Sanitation. It was the local garbage company. Chico's Bail Bonds had nothing on us. We stunk most of the time, and we talked a lot of trash.

Ha!) George got on base, and as usual, I wanted him. I wanted him sooo bad. I threw to first after every pitch, trying to pick him off. Somehow he got to second base. He taunted me, walking around off the bag, looking at me and laughing. I was mad. He just stood out there, between second and third base talking about me and to me. It was unbearable.

Well I had had it. I made up my mind that after the next pitch I was going to charge him. Yeah that's right, charge him. After the next pitch, I came out from behind home plate and sprinted toward George, who was casually walking around, this time he had his back to me. Too bad. By the time he turned around, I was all over him. My actions shocked him—as well as everyone at the park. The only thing he could do was duck. I hit him so hard we both went flying. By the time the dust settled, the umpire (totally shocked) called him out. Yes, "Y'er out!" Great play, Krauss!

My baseball career came to a screeching halt when our high school baseball coach, "Swede" Hatfield, called me down in front of the rest of the team. I should have thanked him, but he died a couple of years ago. It started when, being somewhat cocky again, I went to him in confidence and told him I was ready to start—as were a couple of the other players he had benched. Well, in front of the team he called me out.

"Barry Krauss thinks he is better than everyone else on this team, and we are not going to tolerate this kind of conduct!" He let everyone know that if we were ever going to win, we had to have players that were not self-centered like I was. He dismissed the team after making an example of me. At that moment I told him I was done. I quit.

Baseball was over for me. It was a sad ending to a game I loved.

Even sadder was the fact that I didn't realize what I had done. I had approached this man as an adult—almost an equal—a fact he obviously didn't appreciate.

He made a huge negative impact on me. Like all lessons, you can take what you want from them.

At the time, it only made me reluctant to trust coaches and adults.

The second part of the lesson came to me years later under Coach Bryant: if you have someone who believes in you and encourages you, there is nothing you cannot achieve. It only takes one coach saying the wrong thing, at the wrong time, to discourage someone, to end a career.

Thank God for all of my good coaches. And thank God for Coach Bryant. Twenty-five years after leaving Alabama, I'm still learning from him. Throughout my adulthood there have been times when I have experienced a situation that triggers a flashback to something he told me—which at the time meant nothing to me—and its significance strikes me like a lightning bolt.

As long as there is one person alive who has played under Coach Bryant, he is still teaching.

3

The University of Alabama, Paul "Bear" Bryant, and Me

To understand how a Florida boy like me could choose Alabama over much larger Florida schools, all you have to do is travel back in time.

For those of you who don't have a time machine or aren't old enough to remember those times—and those who are *plenty old* but can't remember them now anyway—let me take you back to those days.

For starters, in the 1960s and 1970s, if any football team in America was going to win the NCAA National Football Championship, it had to come through Alabama.

The decade of the 1960s had Coach Bryant and Alabama either winning outright or sharing three national titles, '61, '64, and '65. Players like Joe Willie Namath and Kenny "The Snake" Stabler had the Tide in the hunt throughout the decade.

Alabama was always there at the top of the heap in some fashion. According to RollTide.com, Alabama's official sports Web site, there are at least five other championships:

> In addition to the 12 "recognized" national championships owned by Alabama, the Official NCAA Football Records Book recognizes Alabama as producing national champions in 1945, 1962, 1966, 1975 and 1977. In 1945, the 10-0 Tide was recognized as champions with Army by the National Championship Foundation. The 1962 Crimson Tide, 10-1, was chosen by Billingsley and Sagarin, while the 1966 team, 11-0, was selected by Berryman. The 11-1 Tide team in 1975, along with Ohio State, was selected by Matthews. In 1977, Football Research picked Alabama, 11-1, and Notre Dame as co-national champions.

As exhibited by the national championship voting trends of the 1960s, sportswriters in national media centers voted their regional favorites above Alabama if at all possible—even back in 1961 when the Tide went undefeated and shared the championship with Ohio State.

The Coaches' Poll was much the same.

Still, the great teams—Southern Cal, Notre Dame, UCLA, Ohio State—all knew that if they were going to actually *win* a national championship, they would have to beat Alabama.

By the time I hit high school, I was a huge fan of the Alabama Crimson Tide. My friends and I took our footballs to the beach and practiced the wishbone—smashing into Mother Nature's waves in our imaginary dives for pay dirt. We loved Alabama. We loved the fact that they would grind and grind, and finally when the opposing team thought they had the run solved, Richard Todd would hit Ozzie Newsome for a sixty-five-yard touchdown. Dammit, they were great.

In my junior and senior years of high school—the 1973 and 1974 football seasons—Alabama again came within one single puff of Coach Bryant's unfiltered Chesterfield cigarette of winning two national championships. The culprit both years—Notre Dame, in bowl games.

So, when I got my first letter from Alabama, I was ecstatic. But my ecstasy was soon dampened by my best friend. "You'll never be good enough to play at Alabama," he said.

I'll never forget those words. They reinforced my resolve. I need to go back and thank him.

Any doubts I had about my goals were overcome by my enthusiasm, fired by a trip to Miami. The University of Miami made the mistake of inviting me down for an official visit when they played Alabama in 1974. I jumped all over that opportunity.

I couldn't wait to meet Coach Bryant and see Kenny Martin, my recruiter from Alabama. I used that game to really study Alabama up-close. And believe me, they were *awesome!* They killed Miami that day, much worse than the score of 28–7 indicated, if I remember correctly. When I left, all I could think about was Alabama. If I ever got the opportunity, I would be a Crimson Tider. Wow!

My dream came true on the night of my high school's Athletic Banquet. I came home after the dinner and walked in to see Paul "Bear" Bryant standing in my living room. How my parents had pulled it off without me knowing something, I still do not understand. I signed with Alabama that night, as soon as "The Man" put the paperwork in front of me.

We all hit it off great. Before he left, my mom was wearing Coach Bryant's houndstooth hat and kidding around with the greatest football coach of all time. I was deliriously happy.

Of course, again, my best friend tried to shoot me down. "You're never gonna get to play there." He was on his way to being traded in after that comment.

Above: Mrs. Krauss borrows Coach Bryant's hat on the day Barry signed with Alabama. (*Miami Herald* staff photo by John Copeland)

University of Alabama Assistant Coach Kenny Martin, Coach Bryant, Barry, Jim Vanover (Barry's high school coach), and Alabama Assistant Coach Lewis Campbell celebrate Barry's signing. (*Miami Herald* staff photo by John Copeland)

Flanked by his mom and dad, Barry signs with Alabama on December 19, 1974. (*Miami Herald* Staff photo by John Copeland)

First Day as a Crimson Tider

In 1975, on the hottest mid-August day since the Earth first cooled, I reported to the University of Alabama. Our first meeting as a team was in an upstairs theatre-style classroom in what was then known as Memorial Coliseum, on the day before we began two-a-day practices.

Looking back now, I see that the whole first meeting scenario was pretty contrived. All scholarship players and a few select walk-ons were there. The assistant coaches immediately laid out the rules—dos and don'ts—and the big rule. Coach Bryant is "The Man." They actually called him "The Man."

Then, on cue, "The Man" walked into our lives. He talked briefly about what he expected, then asked each of us to stand up, tell everyone our names, where we were from, and our position.

He was charming and witty and quick to growl an almost unrecognizable comment. All of us being new to his low, rumbling voice, we had to listen hard to understand anything he said.

Coach Bryant told one player, Joe Moore—now my writing partner—that he needed a haircut . . . "before practice tomorrow." Now remember, we had to check in for practice at 5:00 a.m., and it was already about 8:30 p.m. Joe drove 130 miles round-trip that night to have his mother cut his hair. At 5 a.m. the next morning, every coach noticed. It was one of the most admired haircuts ever—just for its sheer defiance of the time-space continuum.

When Coach Bryant left the meeting that night, we realized this college football thing was purely professional. The assistant coaches broke us up into position meetings, and we immediately started work on the rudimentary tasks we would be expected to know the following morning.

ALMOST AN EX-CRIMSON TIDER

For me, just having the chance to go to Alabama, to play Division I football, was a chance of a lifetime.

Little did I know, God was going to give me (most probably because He knew I could use all the help I could get) at least three more equally dramatic chances just while I was at Alabama.

But I almost blew it.

It all started with the Southern Mississippi game in Birmingham on October 9, 1976, in my sophomore year. We had beaten them 24–8 in a very sloppy game by Alabama standards. Five fumbles, missed tackles, horrible blocking execution—we just stunk it up.

Of course, it was a win, and we were whooping it up in the locker room until Coach Bryant came in—in a very bad mood. The room chilled as soon as we noticed his face. He gave us a good chewing out and called a meeting for the minute we hit Bryant Hall, the football dorm, back in Tuscaloosa.

After a totally silent bus ride (an hour and a half), we pulled up to the dorm and filed into the cafeteria. Coach Bryant came in and made it short and sweet.

"As far as I'm concerned," Coach Bryant drawled, "we're done playing football this year."

Our performance was so pitiful, he said, that he would call the NCAA and cancel the rest of the season. He was that mad. Of course, he then put the monkey on our backs.

"You players decide among yourselves, right now, if we're gonna play out the rest of the season. If we are, you all are gonna have to change your attitudes and commit to working harder on the fundamentals."

With that he told us he would wait outside for our decision and left the room.

In only a moment we called him back in and told him we wanted to play.

"Fine, then, we'll be on the field tomorrow at 6 a.m."

Bear Bryant had just called a Sunday practice. After a win, no less.

Looking back, it is easy to see Coach Bryant's quandary. We had lost the first game of the season to Ole Miss, 10–7, in a major fluke. They played over their heads and got one huge break, which allowed them to win. The week prior to Southern Miss, we had been shut out by Georgia, 21–0. So this Alabama team had been 2-2 going into the game against Southern Mississippi. Coach was expecting a turnaround, and what he got was this horrible, sloppy performance.

To top it off, the next week was the Tennessee game in Knoxville. A loss to Tennessee could put us in a nosedive that could end up giving Alabama a losing season. He had to get our attention right then. He had to turn this team around that very moment. The rest of the season would only get harder—we had LSU, Notre Dame, and Auburn as our last three games.

Obviously, when the meeting in Bryant Hall was over, we were all on a tremendous downer. But the campus was alive and kicking, since we had won.

Skip Ramsey, a quarterback from Georgia who was in my class, and I decided to walk down what was called New Fraternity Row. It was within a stone's throw of Bryant Hall, and we could take in some of the local color at the game-day parties before we jumped back on the football bandwagon Sunday morning.

Strike One!

Well, we found a fraternity house that was having a great party and proceeded to drink free beer for several hours. We probably even tried to snake a couple of dates but with no success.

At around 10:55 I looked at Skip. Curfew was at 11:00, and we could barely make it if we hurried. "Should we go?" I asked.

"Are you playing?" Skip responded, obviously not happy with riding the pine, a feeling I shared.

"No!" I blurted.

Decision made.

Strike Two!

We were having way too much fun to go home, particularly with that Sunday morning practice hanging over our heads.

Unbeknownst to us, the greatest football coach of all time had chosen that night to drive home his point about attitude and commitment. For the first time anyone could remember, Bear Bryant did a bed check in the dorm after curfew.

Strike Three!

When I showed up at the locker room bright and early Sunday morning, everyone was just staring at me. Finally someone asked if I knew how much trouble I was in.

"What are you talking about?"

"Coach Bryant did room check last night," he said.

My world imploded at that moment.

My teammate added helpfully, "The last guy he caught never played another down at Alabama." I couldn't go any lower.

Now I was really scared. An incredible sickness overwhelmed my body. My throat sank into my stomach. I became ill. Sick! Nauseated! I wanted to cry I felt so bad. But I didn't know what to do other than get dressed and get out on the field.

Over the next two-and-one-half hours I had probably thirty people tell me, "It's over for you, Krauss."

My good friend Marty Lyons had no advice when I asked him what to do.

"I would hate to be you!" he responded. Isn't that great? From my best friend, too.

Practice was very intense. The Bear was making his point. There was a lot of hitting. A lot. I remember not playing much. The coaches, the players, the team managers—everyone—basically ignored me. That is when you know you are in a lot of trouble in football . . . when they quit talking to you. They quit yelling at you.

The words of my best friend in high school rang in my ears. "You're not going to make it."

As I stood there and watched practice, I thought of how I had blown it—my opportunity to play Division I, big-time football, was over. I knew it.

And it was my own fault. No one else's. Not Skip's. Not anyone's, other than mine.

Sick as a dog and feeling doomed to my fate, I asked a coach what I should do. I was in such a funk I don't even remember who it was. He suggested that I go and meet with Coach Bryant and beg. I thought he was joking.

After practice I went back to the dorm and thought about what I had done . . . and wallowed in some self-pity. My friend was right. I wasn't good enough. I didn't have the discipline needed to play at this level. I didn't have the ability. I didn't have the commitment. I didn't have any luck, couldn't catch a break . . .

In the middle of that self-flagellation I had a revelation. Maybe I could save myself, just maybe. Maybe I *should* go see Coach Bryant. The coach, whoever he was, was right!

It was my last chance, and I had to do it. This defining moment, going to see Coach Bryant, was the stuff that legends were made of at Alabama. Everyone knew the stories of Joe Namath and Kenny Stabler. Both got suspended—they both missed curfew, and Coach Bryant hammered them. And they were two good-looking guys, quarterbacks, important to the team. Oh, my God, what was he going to do to an ugly linebacker like me. Hell there was no telling how many players like me had their helmets and their scalps lifted right there in his office. At the same time. But I had to do it.

I realized that because of his Sunday television-show commitments that Bryant couldn't see me that afternoon, and that he probably wouldn't kick me off the team until Monday, so I made up my mind to catch him as early as possible Monday morning.

Bright and early the next day I took a seat at the receptionist's desk on the top floor of Memorial Coliseum. I was sure Coach Bryant had been in the building—but not in his office—several hours by that time.

I heard him first. He was walking—shuffling would be more accurate. Then I saw him: khaki pants over untied, muddy boots, with a flannel shirt. He wore an old beat up Alabama cap that looked like it had spent several decades in a damp, dark basement under a pile of clothes.

As he got closer, I stood up in front of him. I was shaking in my shoes when I asked if I could speak with him for a moment. He agreed with a nod of his head, and I followed him into his office.

Now you have to visualize this office. It was dramatic—fit for a corporate chieftain or the greatest football coach of all time: dark wood paneling, a big desk in the middle of the room covered with piles of papers and books, and things on the wall that were really important.

He sat in his chair behind the massive desk—definitely *the* power position—and pointed me to the couch.

As I sat down, I realized it was a big mistake: I sank into the sofa. Looking back on it, I'm sure that sinking sofa has held many a sinking player. It was the ultimate psychological tool.

It hit me as a metaphor for what was happening—sinking into oblivion under the gaze of God.

I jumped up and began to blurt out my apology. I yammered on for a moment, then stopped.

Coach Bryant had his head down—perhaps working on something super important, but it could have been he was playing tic-tac-toe—and he never looked at me. The room was dead quiet. I started talking again, but under this much pressure I folded.

Here I am, an invincible nineteen-year-old who has just realized he is only human after all.

I started pleading my case again, but he still never looked up. He ignored me. I probably said something else like, "I am sorry coach for what I have done. I feel you are not giving me the chance I thought you were going to give me. I made a mistake, and I am sorry."

Coach Bryant said nothing. He didn't move. He never looked at me. That's when I *knew* I was in deep trouble.

I lost it altogether.

At that time I broke down. I started crying as I continued my story. I said that I felt terrible and that it wouldn't ever happen again.

That wasn't working either.

Did you ever hear of an athlete taking his game to another level? Well that is what I did, although it wasn't exactly planned. The next thing I knew I was crying in convulsions, taking crying to another level. I started jerking all over the place: snot, boogers, and all kinds of liquids were streaming down my face. It was nasty. And it was going all over the place, especially on his desk.

Did you ever lose your breath when you were crying? I did. I was jerking and crying, and, well, you get the idea. It was an ugly sight.

Then I sniffed out my last statement . . . my last-ditch effort to save myself.

"If you kick me out of the dorm and take away my scholarship, my mom is going to kill me!"

Then I just stood there. And stood there . . . and stood there. Until I thought I might explode, not realizing that I was being nuked by the greatest of all psychological manipulators. He had bled me completely dry.

He finally looked up at me.

"Son, you'd better straighten up," he said, and then looked back down to his work. ,

"Yes sir," I said as I ran out of his office. In fact, I didn't stop running until I hit Bryant Hall, where I dove into my bed and continued to cry into my pillow.

And I prayed for mercy. I promised God this would never happen again if He would take care of me. I believe He heard me.

How did I know?

I learned years later that Coaches Clem Gryska and Jack Rutledge had both called my mom, to let my parents know what was going to happen. I was definitely going to be kicked out of the dorm. Coach Bryant had not made up his mind about whether I could stay on the team.

Skip Ramsey missed that Sunday's practice. He did eventually go to see Coach Bryant. He tried to explain his side of the story and save his scholarship. Coach Bryant listened to his story but kicked him out of the dorm anyway. Skip managed to save his scholarship for the time being, but he never got another real shot at playing at Alabama.

What I took away from that episode was simple: Coach Bryant saw something in me that no one else saw—not my coaches, my friends, my family, not anyone. I think that's the part God did.

God stepped in again, in the locker room just before the Notre Dame game in South Bend later that year.

A Big Chance under Touchdown Jesus

Alabama vs. Notre Dame, 1976

The locker room on that day in South Bend was creepy. I had never seen a football team this quiet. We could almost even hear the Four Horsemen through the walls, moving around the Notre Dame locker room.

Coach Bryant was stalking—just pacing back and forth in front of us. Those of us who really knew him were just trying to hide; it seemed like a pre-explosion situation. The resulting player tension was evident in eyes all around the room as they followed Coach's movements.

"Krauss, hey Krauss," he suddenly yelled, not knowing where I was.

"Man, what did I do now?" was my first thought. Something made me jump up and hustle through the crowded locker room, the pitiful object of dozens of frozen stares. I'm sure they were all thinking, "Well, *this* is it for Krauss, this time for sure."

I ran up to Coach Bryant and the other coaches standing close to the locker room door. They were extremely nervous—this was supposed to be where we avenged the two national championship losses to this same Notre Dame team.

I didn't notice the official until Coach turned to him.

"This man wants to talk to you," pointing to the lead official.

I searched Coach Bryant's eyes, only to see no emotion. Yet I knew he was furious inside.

The official pulled out a black-and-white photograph of what looked like a baseball team. "Does anyone in this picture look familiar?"

I couldn't believe this. This guy from nowhere is quizzing me in front of *all* of our coaches. What could I do? What could Coach Bryant do?

Well, before the biggest game of the year and possibly the decade, you let the lead official have his say.

"How about this guy?" the official went on. "He's your father."

I stared at the old photo. Hell, he was right. The guy went on to talk about how he had played with and coached my father on an Illinois Bell company softball team in Chicago.

"Your dad was a pretty good player," he went on to say, smiling and slapping me on the back.

If looks could kill, I'd have been dead at the beginning of the conversation, the assistant coaches the executioners. They were incredulous. I was scared to death. Everyone put up with the guy—until he finished—by now almost a cigarette full of Chesterfield ashes hung from Coach Bryant's lips. He, too, was flabbergasted.

But something about that moment hung in Coach Bryant's mind.

Well, in the second quarter one of our linebackers missed an open-field tackle—that was Coach's unpardonable sin for linebackers—and I heard his roar over the sidelines, the bands, and the crowd. "Krauss, get in there!"

Not to be too redundant, but this was Notre Dame, at Notre Dame, with the mosaic of Touchdown Jesus on the Library, just outside of one end zone. Now, since the stadium has been expanded, it's not as easy to see from the field—a huge psychological advantage given up for the sake of the almighty dollar. I was a sophomore who had not been getting substantial playing time—except on special teams—against any opponent. This was big! From the time I packed my travel bags to the moment he yelled my name, I had no idea I would get in the game. I wasn't even expecting to sniff the field. Coach Bryant made that call. *Yelled* the call! I didn't have time to think about how big this opportunity was; I only thought about playing—wide open.

My career turned around that day. But the exact moment was not on the field; it was in the locker room at halftime. After Coach Bryant finished with his instructions, the place went silent for a moment.

"I want the same starting lineups," he growled, "except I want Krauss in there because he wants to hit somebody."

Talk about a field promotion! I didn't give a damn who was on the library wall. I was on a rampage. Bear Bryant gave me the reins and told me to go. He made me a football player at that moment!

We wound up losing, 21–18—they picked us off in the end zone as we were about to score for the come-from-behind win—but I had a game to die for. I ended up with eighteen tackles, an interception, and a forced fumble that day. I was all over the field. It was just my day, or maybe they hadn't seen much film on me, or didn't bother working up a scheme against me.

It wasn't until years later that I realized what an alignment of the stars had to take place for those things to happen. Just another day at the office for the Man Upstairs and his proxy on Earth, Bear Bryant.

I told my dad of the incident after the game. He looked up the list of game officials and realized the man who came into the locker room was Bob Fallan, the referee. Fallan had been an installer/repairman with my dad at Illinois Bell in Chicago, prior to my parents moving to Pompano. They had not talked for years prior to the game, so Mr. Fallan had obviously made the connection between my father and me on his own, dug out the picture, and approached Coach Bryant. Perhaps most interesting, my family had been in Pompano since before I was born, so it had been at least twenty years since he had seen my dad.

Talk about tricky connections.

As a college kid, I didn't care how it had come about. I just wanted to play.

After this almost inexplicable incident at Notre Dame, I started every game for the remainder of my career. And for the rest of that season I was on a roll.

The next game was Auburn, in the Iron Bowl, at Legion Field in Birmingham. A great place for my first start. As always, Auburn played over their heads against us, but we managed to kick their asses anyway, 38-7. I had another great day, eighteen tackles. Everywhere I went, there was an Auburn guy with the ball. All I had to do was execute—football has never been more fun. Bob Baumhower had a career game, too—fifteen tackles, some hurries, and a bucketful of intimidation and general destruction. He was almost single-handedly responsible for turning their offensive line into grits that day—he just waded through them.

Then, to cap off a pretty good year, came the Liberty Bowl.

The Liberty Bowl—Memphis, Tennessee

UCLA vs. Alabama, December 20, 1976

The Auburn game had been only two weeks earlier, and we were still riding pretty high.

As the date neared we heard a little about the weather. When the day arrived, the weather was the dominant story.

Whoa, Nellie, was it cold. And windy. People started fires in the stands. There were stories of folks spilling drinks on their clothes and having it turn to ice in just moments.

Standing on the sidelines before the game, I was psyched. Then there was a huge fireworks display, which for some reason just sent me into orbit.

We kicked off. I'm not sure what happened—could have been an extremely high kick, or adrenaline, or loving to play in cold weather—but I outran everybody down the field, dodged every UCLA blocker, and just *exploded* the receiver as soon as he caught it and took a step. Just one-on-one and I killed him. That first play set the tone of the game. It was one of those "once-in-a-lifetime" hits. Our defense was so fired up the boys from Westwood didn't have a chance.

Charlie Hannah, our big defensive lineman who eventually played for the Tampa Bay Buccaneers and the Oakland Raiders, tipped a pass, which I intercepted and ran back forty-four yards for a touchdown.

Everyone played great—on offense, defense, and special teams. And again, this was on national television. Alabama, 36–6!

After the game I stood on the frozen turf of the Liberty Bowl with Coach Bryant (he had a scarf over his head and face) and accepted the Liberty Bowl MVP and Defensive Player of the Game awards. Coach Bryant accepted the Winner's Trophy. Some of the regional newspapers ran the photo of us together. What a thrill and an honor it was to stand there with him after that victory.

My career, at least in the media, skyrocketed.

4

Learning Life, and Football, from a Living Legend

"Coach Bryant taught us about life," said Byron Braggs, a great defensive tackle on our 1977–80 teams. "He taught his assistants about football, and made it their job to teach us."

Byron is exactly right. Although we didn't know it then, this was just another of the ways Coach prioritized what we learned. He knew the really important lessons were about life, not football.

Every day I am reminded of at least one of his lessons. In today's complex world, decades removed from those wonderful, carefree days at Alabama, there are times when I experience something and immediately have a flashback to a meeting or a conversation with Coach Bryant. "Ah ha," I think. "That's what he meant!"

As long as one of his players is still alive, he is still coaching.

Interestingly, different players took different lessons from Coach Bryant. He knew how to give each individual what he needed. Just like he knew there was something special inside of me when I was more of a liability than an asset to the team.

THE BIGGEST LESSON

Coach Bryant did have some universal lessons that were taught to everyone— sometimes in very different ways. His biggest lesson in life and football was simple: Never quit.

Yes, there were other commandments, like "always call your momma," and "always show your class," on which other lessons were built. But the big lesson was "never quit."

This is one of the greatest ironies of playing football at the University of Alabama. Coach Bryant wanted to make you quit. He worked you so hard that you wanted to quit. If you had any thought of quitting in you, he wanted to get it out and get rid of it, or he wanted you to get off his football field. Everyone who ever played for him was challenged. There was no praise, no positive reinforcement: You could quit at any time. He gave you many reasons and every opportunity.

There was no place for quitters on his team.

If you quit in practice, he knew you'd quit in a game, and that's the last thing in the world Coach Bryant would tolerate.

The Quitter Test/AKA the Personal Gut Check

There was only one way to make sure that every individual on the team was not a quitter—the Quitter Test. Obviously, this wasn't a standardized test that required a No. 2 Ticonderoga pencil and machine-readable computer answer card or an interview with a psychologist. This test was unique to Coach Paul "Bear" Bryant. In true Bear Bryant form he knew exactly how to test each of us . . . how to know if we would ever quit. The quitter test for some was simple—he watched us every day in practice, then looked deep into our souls, and knew immediately if we were ever susceptible to quitting. For others he needed tangible proof.

For Rickey Gilliland, a kid from Birmingham who played my position, "the quitter test" came in our sophomore year—supposedly Rickey's red-shirt year. As discussed earlier, Coach Bryant was white-hot mad at our performance against Southern Miss and called a Sunday morning practice. Of course, later Coach Bryant was also disgusted with me and needed to find someone to step up into my special teams role if he kicked me off the team. Rickey had a great practice that Sunday and caught Coach Bryant's eye. He worked hard all week, and at one point Coach Paul Crane approached him. "Get ready, you're in at Tennessee," he said.

He went in on the third defensive play of the game, played most of the game, and graded out a winner. The following Monday he was kicked back down the depth chart. Obviously disappointed, Rickey was again approached by Coach Crane—out of school, of course—who offered a hint of encouragement. "Work hard this week in practice," was all he offered.

Rickey worked hard and had a great week—even though he was listed as second team every day on the depth chart. On Saturday Rickey Gilliland was announced as a starter for the Louisville game.

Coach Crane took Rickey aside later in the season and told him that Coach Bryant was "checking his oil" that week. He thought Rickey might "quit mentally" in the face of his treatment.

Marty Lyons's test was a bit more dramatic.

Controlled scrimmages were a favorite of Coach Bryant. The assistant coaches would switch out players between plays in this full-speed game-type scrimmage. It was wide open. After about six or eight plays, you started looking toward your position coach to pull you.

On this particular day it became apparent that Marty was being put to the test. He started, he played, and he was never pulled. Players came and went, came and went, but Marty stayed. Toward the end—maybe eighty or ninety plays—his eyes were glassed over, he was bloody, and he was soaked with sweat . . . but he never quit.

E. J. Junior had much the same kind of test, except it went farther.

"In the spring of my sophomore year I was coming off an injury," said Junior. "We were having a controlled scrimmage and the coaches wanted me to start out slowly, so they put me in at strong safety first. Then they started moving me around until I finally got back to defensive end."

"We kept going and going . . . I couldn't hold my arms up I was so tired," he said through a wry smile. "We got to 90 plays, then 100. On about play 110, I made it into the backfield and hit someone hard, but I didn't have the energy to wrap my arms around him and complete the tackle."

Coach Bryant yelled down from his usual position in the tower by the practice field, "Hey, there's someone trying to be another E. J. Junior."

"Coach," responded Defensive Coach Ken Donahue, "that is E. J."

"Hell, Coach," Bear Bryant answered, "I thought I took him out on play 75! Get out of there, E. J.!"

"You never know how much you can do until you get pushed," Junior says today. "We all got pushed."

David Hannah's story is one of betrayal, character, perseverance, and ultimately victory—two national championships.

"As a freshman," relates David, "I got moved up to the varsity quickly and played in the offensive line. However, at some point in the season a coach went to Coach Bryant and told him, 'David Hannah is a wasted scholarship.' Ken Donahue was in the room and immediately responded, 'I'll take him!'

"That was the greatest disappointment in my life up to that point," David continues. "But it was also inspiring. Coach Paul Crane came up to me and said, 'David, you can do one of two things—you can prove it's true, or you can make a liar and a joke out of him.'

"At that moment," says David, "I had a goal. Coach Crane committed to helping me learn the defensive line position and techniques which would give me the experience I needed to play. The next year I was red-shirted as I tried to learn the position. Wiley Barnes and I would meet with Coach Crane for twenty or thirty minutes after every practice, going over thousands of things to help us learn the position."

E. J. Junior's Side-BEAR Story

Every player at Alabama had as one of his primary goals becoming a starter, even before he ever put on a pad. It was something we were all working toward. In practice, being a starter meant wearing a white jersey if you were a defensive player, or a red jersey as an offensive player.

I remember vividly the day I became a starter. It was the week after we had lost to Nebraska in my freshman year, 1977. That day I wasn't having a particularly good practice. I happened to look up and see Coach Bryant coming down from his tower.

"Oh, no!" I thought.

Coach Bryant only came down out of the tower for one of four reasons (outside of lightning): there was a dignitary on the field; someone was hurt; he was going to chew someone out; or practice was over. I did some quick checking—no dignitary, no one hurt, the day was clear, and it was way too early to end practice. As he hit the ground, he started heading for me. I was about to realize my greatest nightmare.

He walked squarely up to me—face-to-face—and said, "E. J. Junior, go grab a white jersey and join the starters."

I was so dumbfounded, I just stood there.

"Didn't you hear what I said, son?" he growled loudly.

I tore out toward the equipment man and got my white jersey on.

Later, eight years into my professional football career, my mother told me that she was there for that moment. It seems that Coach Bryant had called her and told her what was going to happen.

She came all the way to Tuscaloosa from Nashville and was standing in the entrance to the tunnel from our locker room, watching the whole thing.

David's commitment paid off in both 1978 and 1979, in being a member of two national championship teams.

Never quit!

There is nothing more indicative of the power of this lesson than "The Goal Line Stand." Some of the football experts in the stands, the press box, and even some coaches on the field that New Year's Day say they were already thinking about how quickly our offense could come back from the imminent touchdown Penn

State was about to score. Yet I can tell you right now, there was never any doubt in any of our minds that we would stop the most dominant college football team in the country as we ran back on to the turf of the Superdome.

Not one quitter in the bunch. Not even one thought of quitting. It was "Gut Check" time. We all knew what the situation meant. We had all been through it before, hundreds or thousands of times in practice. No sir. No way.

Thank you, Coach Bryant!

Almost every player at Alabama talks about the work ethic instilled by Coach Bryant.

Rich Wingo, my friend and fellow middle linebacker on the Superdome turf that day, says those lessons have carried him throughout his professional football career and real life.

"The harder you work, the more success you have," says Rich. "We had worked all of our college careers for that moment. Some people give something a try, find it harder than they expect, and then rationalize getting out or quitting. You are either a winner, or you aren't. And you carry those habits through life."

Coach Bryant also taught me to be courageous in the face of great odds and to stand up for what was right.

Those lessons paid off when I got into the NFL.

The National Football League is a different place. The first year I was with the Baltimore Colts we lost more games than I experienced in my entire career at Alabama—we went 5-11. I realized how important those lessons were.

Personnel battles, management changes, coaching changes, new offensive and defensive schemes: the professional ranks are constantly in a state of flux. Personally, you have to have a foundation, a strong belief in yourself and in doing what you know is right. Without Coach Paul Bear Bryant's lessons I, like many professionals, would have been adrift in a sea of confusion.

The Frank Kush era with the Colts was my greatest test.

When the Baltimore Colts went to camp in 1982, the first thing our new head coach, Frank Kush, told all the players was to call him "Coach," never Frank.

Frank already had the reputation of an abusive coach—he had slugged a punter on his Arizona State team. That incident had made national news. We were pretty apprehensive about this new adventure.

We were right.

Frank Kush didn't give respect, and he didn't get respect. After so many years in the college ranks, he didn't realize that professional players have a different mental outlook. Professional players are just that. They take on a serious attitude about their jobs, put a good work ethic in place, and treat their time on the field as their profession.

Frank Kush treated men like they were still kids. He would try to intimidate players, even physically abuse them, to get them to do things his way. That behavior had been reinforced at Arizona State because he had won with it. But it was destined for failure at this level.

In his first camp he tried to run us into the ground. We would go two-a-days, morning and afternoon, then—after the last practice—he would make us run a mile in the woods.

He would humiliate players at every opportunity. He would even fire players out on the field.

Frank, however, would learn a valuable lesson by firing Holden Smith, from Cal-Berkley. Smith had pulled a hamstring early one day in practice and was in a lot of pain. Coach Kush demanded he run sprints with us at the end of the day. Smith complied, but was dragging.

"OK," Kush said, "everybody has to run an extra five sprints because of Holden Smith."

The players responded negatively, saying Smith was hurt. A couple of sprints later Kush yelled out at Smith, "Hey, you're fired! Get off of my football field! Go on!"

Frank Kush wanted to embarrass and humiliate him.

At dinner later that night I found myself standing at the soda machine next to Holden Smith. "Holden," I said, "I'm sorry about what happened out there today."

"Oh, yeah," Smith responded, "watch this!"

He filled a huge cup with some kind of drink, walked over to the coaches' table, and loudly made an announcement, "All right everybody, can I have your attention please? I want to make sure that Frank Kush understands that he can't treat players like this and get away with it." Then he dumped that huge drink over Kush's head.

Frank jumped up from the table as if to challenge Holden, who immediately got into his face.

"What are you gonna do, Frank, hit me?"

The stalemate went on for a few seconds until assistant coaches jumped in, and the two were separated. We all thought it was over.

Holden walked away, straight back to the drink machine and refilled the cup. Instantly he went back to the coaches' table and sprayed the whole coaching staff, drenching them all. It was a challenge to which none of the coaches responded.

Frank knew he had lost control of the situation. He knew the general consensus was against him. He was in the middle of a bunch of very big men and his intimidation was not working any more. He was getting paid back.

The coaches talked Frank into retreating to his room, but the issue was not yet settled. At about 7:00 that night, as the defense was on the way to one of our meetings, I heard a disturbance. Holden Smith was at Frank's door, trying to kick it down.

"I'm not done with you yet, Frank. Come on out of there," Smith went on. "I'm going to kick your ass!"

Within the hour the local police arrived to escort Holden Smith away from Frank Kush's room. Frank was still in hiding.

Smith, a gifted athlete and artist, left football. Frank, unfortunately, didn't learn enough from this event. Even more unfortunately, he didn't get fired.

In 1984, our first year in Indianapolis, we were on our third year of degradation and insulting behavior by our supposed leader. He had lost all purpose, lost all of his focus. And we lost a lot of games.

The perfect example occurred on a road game at Miami. We had flown in early the day before the game. The team members were focused, as usual, on the game and what we had to do to win it. That afternoon Frank Kush came into a team meeting and began to berate us about how dirty the airplane was when we arrived. He went on about our being slobs for almost thirty minutes.

The whole season was a steady stream of abuse.

The climactic incident for me came on a Saturday walk-through practice, prior to a Sunday game. As anyone who has ever played football knows, these last practices are meant to be positive, morale-building sessions, bringing the team together to get the coming job done.

At the end of these walk-through practices we would jump into our two-minute offense and move the ball down the field against the defense. On this day, when the offense got to the goal line there was an interception.

Frank Kush put on his snidest face. "Great. We just lost another game."

He walked off the practice field—ending practice on that huge downer.

Finally I had had enough. After practice I walked straight into his office, stood in his face, and delivered him a message.

"I'm done with you, Frank. I'm tired of the way you treat everyone. I'm done!"

"Who the hell are you talking to?" he screamed back.

"I'm talking to you. Cut me or fire me," I said.

"I'll tell you when you're fired!" Kush sputtered in reply.

"Do it now, damn it." I yelled, slamming my fist on the table.

I turned to walk away and noticed all the coaches cowering about the locker room.

Later that week Frank Kush got fired. Champagne popped all over Indianapolis—in the homes of coaches, players, and fans.

Hal Hunter was named interim head coach, and he immediately asked if I'd be his team captain.

"I'd be honored," I responded, knowing he appreciated my part in ending the Kush era.

Having the determination, the will, and the courage to stand up to Frank Kush came through me directly from Bear Bryant.

Marty Lyons's Side-BEAR Story

"I learned a world of things just being around Coach Bryant," said Marty Lyons. "There are things a college kid just doesn't understand . . . about life and the importance of relationships, which Coach Bryant taught us without us even knowing it.

"When you have some devastating experience later in life, those lessons come back to you. It really happened for me in 1982, when in a matter of days I had three huge events: my son was born on March 4, my Dad died on March 8, and a friend's child was diagnosed with leukemia on March 10.

"The power of these events was staggering, each life-changing in its own way. But coming all together, I was totally overwhelmed. It was one of those times when I turned back to some of Coach Bryant's lessons.

"Without his lessons on life and relationships, I would have had a very difficult time with those events. I didn't quit, I didn't give up. Instead, I responded the only way I knew how—by throwing myself into solving a problem. I formed a foundation which funds the wishes of terminally ill children. It is still active today, and I am extremely proud of our work."

Mike Clements, who played defensive back at Alabama with me, also remembers Coach Bryant as a great actor. Mike recalls a meeting during bowl practice leading up to the Sugar Bowl where Coach Bryant talked about one of his favorite subjects—Gut Check. This time it was presented in the form of a metaphor.

"In a display which was, to my knowledge, pretty rare," Mike says, "Coach Bry-

Byron Braggs Side-BEAR Story

"Coach Bryant always said we were special," said Braggs.

"'Everyone wants to do it,' he would say during two-a-day practices, 'but not everyone's willing to pay the price.'

"We bought into it," said Byron. "Now it seems second nature to me—he instilled my purpose and work ethic.

"The acting part came with his stories," continues Braggs. "On Wednesday night before the 1980 Tennessee game, Coach Bryant had us in a group meeting. He started on one of his stories, but it wasn't *just* one of his stories. It was a story about the difference between winners and losers. When he finished, everyone in the room was at an emotional zenith. We were all in tears.

"I looked at Mitch Ferguson and he said, 'I have to go kill someone right now.'

"Well, this was a Johnny Majors Tennessee team, and they were having a great year. The game was on national television, and Ara Parsegian was doing the color commentary. When we walked on the field we were ready.

"We beat Tennessee 27–0. They had no first down until the third quarter. At the end of the third quarter—leading 24–0, the fans gave us a standing ovation. Parsegian, who never heaped praise on an Alabama team, actually said, 'I have never seen a team dominated like this.'

"After the game," Byron continues, "came another very special moment in my life. My dad came into the locker room, and I got to light his victory cigar. I will never forget that moment."

ant went to the chalkboard and started drawing—a house. As he drew he talked in metaphors. This house is our team.

'Sometimes,' Coach Bryant said, 'you have to check on things in your house to make sure everything is OK. And sometimes you find that your house has termites.'

"Coach Bryant was drawing on this big chalkboard like some kind of engineer—except his figures were almost cartoonlike.

'And when that wood in the foundation of your house has termites, you have to really treat it aggressively.' Coach continued, 'You have to eliminate all the bad wood—get it out of there. Here we are on the verge of a national championship, and I'm not so sure about our foundation. We haven't had our Gut Check.'

"The players were all enthralled as he went on and on about the bad wood at the foundation," Mike relates. "Then, almost like magic, he went into a discussion of the next spring, like he was dismissing this year's team.

'We're going to have a real Gut Check in the spring,' Coach Bryant promised. 'We'll find out who wants to play football and who is the good wood, and who is the bad wood,' he concluded.

"Seniors on the team approached me after the speech," said Mike, "and talked about how glad they were they were not going to be here with us in the spring.

"Looking back," Mike Clements said, "that was Coach Bryant's way of challenging the seniors—the foundation of the team. He knew exactly what he was doing, he just did it in a way which didn't immediately threaten them, but soundly inspired them.

"The next time I heard the term 'gut check' was from Murray Legg on second down and goal in 'The Goal Line Stand.'"

Mike Clements's Side-BEAR Story

I was on the training table in New Orleans the night before the 1979 Sugar Bowl, watching Ohio State in the Gator Bowl, and Coach Bryant was standing right by me talking to someone. We both saw Woody Hayes slug the Clemson player—an act that effectively ended his career.

The first words out of Coach Bryant's mouth showed his love of his competitors and his understanding of the ramifications of Hayes's actions.

"Isn't that a shame that happened to Woody, that he'd have to go out this way."

Don McNeal, the tremendous defensive back who made the outstanding play on that second down in the goal line stand at the Sugar Bowl, remembers one of Coach Bryant's greatest lessons, as well as his greatest gift to his players, as "confidence."

"You know, it seems simple now," says McNeal, "but we got our confidence from Coach Bryant. He was cool and confident at all times—although it didn't always look like it."

"His confidence was most apparent when things weren't going well, and that happened a lot at the beginning of the 1978 season. I can remember coming in at halftime being down, when nothing had gone right, and he was ultra cool.

"Coach Bryant would say, 'Get a drink, relax, don't get excited . . . We're gonna come back. Here is what we're gonna do.'

"Then we would break up into our offensive, defensive, or special teams groups and go about laying out the plan he put together. When we got back on the field, it was all business. That was Bear Bryant. And even more important, we did it.

"There was no way we wanted to let down this man who so believed in us."

Don McNeal's Side-BEAR Story

When I was growing up in Atmore, Alabama, I was being recruited by almost all of the SEC schools. At the time, we didn't have a phone, but one of our neighbors did. I can still remember it like yesterday; the neighbor would come running, "Don McNeal, you have a telephone call from Coach Bear Bryant!"

"How are your Mama and Daddy?" he would always ask first. And he was sincere. He really wanted to know that everything was okay in the family. After talking about family and football, and seemingly just right before he was ready to hang up, he would tell me that he wanted me at Alabama. I knew this man was sincere. This was his priority in life. What I learned later was that he considered his football players as family.

Coach Bryant taught us thousands of other lessons that we still use today. One I still live every day is "*Never* be late."

Being late for something was the quickest way to get into his doghouse. I was very lucky I learned that early. As a freshman I remember running up the stairs of Memorial Coliseum with Marty Lyons on our way to a team meeting. We were always in competition, so I'm sure we were racing—when we dashed past this old man bent over in the stairwell tying his shoe.

When we hit the classroom, the meeting had already started. Moments later, that old man—Paul W. Bryant—came into the room. I could feel it . . . he was really going to rip into us. He was looking directly at me when the door opened and another player tried to slip into the room. Coach had to divert his attention to this new victim. He really made an example of the guy.

"If the meeting was at 1:30," says Don McNeal, "I would always try to get there by 1:00, because if Coach Bryant was in on it, there was a good chance he'd be there at 1:15, and believe me, that's when the meeting would start."

There was never an excuse for being late. But we sometimes tested fate.

At the 1978 Sugar Bowl, against Ohio State, I almost "bought the big one." Marty and I—is there a pattern here?—were travel roommates and always kept our room like a cave, dark and cold. We wanted it perfect for hibernating. The day before the game the whole team was scheduled for a meeting in the Superdome at 2:00 p.m. For some reason I had slept in that day—way late. At 1:55 my phone rang and awakened me. Marty was reminding me.

I threw on gym shorts and a T-shirt and ran for the elevator. *It took forever.* Once I got downstairs, I ran across the walkway to the Superdome and hustled around the place looking for a door that was open. Once inside I shot downstairs and then heard voices. When I turned the corner, I saw our equipment managers in the hallway, with all of my gear. They helped me dress and I quickly hustled to my place in the front row. As I sat down Coach Bryant turned the corner out of the portal, and the group went quiet.

"Some of you," he began, "think you are better than others."

I cringed. This was it for me. I just knew it.

"Missing curfew is a serious infraction," Coach Bryant continued.

Whew! I almost couldn't hear him for my heart racing. He had caught two guys the night before, out too late on New Year's Eve. They were suspended for the game. I felt as if I had just missed being hit by a bus.

Yet I always wondered about the timing of his entrance, and the miracle of the equipment managers being at exactly the right place at the right time.

During our senior year Marty Lyons, Murray Legg, Rich Wingo, and I were once—for some reason best forgotten—extremely late getting to the locker room. When we walked in, we realized everyone was already dressed and in a meeting in another room. We panicked. There was no way we could walk into a meeting and not be discovered.

We all decided to take our chances rather than give ourselves away. We threw on our gear and went out the tunnel to the field and hid in the bushes lining the fence. When the players came ambling out onto the field, we began to mingle in with them like we were with the group.

Although we were all in fear that there was a comment in the meeting—like "you got that, Krauss?"—we all believe to this day that we miraculously got by with our transgression.

Barry's Side-BEAR Story

Gene Stallings once said to me, "Did you ever notice that Coach always got mad at the perfect time?" Obviously Coach Stallings also believes that Coach Bryant was an excellent actor.

However, Coach Bryant did seem legitimately mad at times.

We were playing a day game at LSU, and Coach Bryant came into the locker room after pregame warm-ups flat-out furious. We assumed it was due to the typical LSU behavior—folks cussing, booing, or maybe even throwing something at him as he took his traditional walk around Tiger Stadium.

We found out later why he was so mad. LSU had switched their "Mike the Tiger" mascots—real tigers—for some reason, death, I suppose, or maybe the first one flunked out. As Coach went over to pet "Mike the Tiger" through the cage, as he customarily had done for several years, the animal tried to attack him, lunging at his arm. Coach was mad that the handlers hadn't told him this was a different Mike.

E. J. Junior always had a special relationship with Coach Bryant. He was constantly dropping by his office, whether it was to talk about last week's game or to ask for help in rescheduling an engineering lab; it didn't matter.

"Coach Bryant's admonitions to 'call your mamas and daddies!' and his inquiries of 'how are your folks?' were sincere. He came to my house as the final step in my recruiting," Junior explains. "He told me and my parents two things: 'At Alabama E. J. will get a quality education—and we'll work his tail off.' Boy, that was what my mother, a school principal, wanted to hear. I was going to Alabama after that. My mother and dad considered him as my 'other father' in Tuscaloosa.

"Coach always knew what was going on in my life," E. J. continues. "He knew who I was dating. He knew everything. When, as a freshman, I was having trouble with a class, he knew that, too. He wanted to help."

E. J. Junior's Side-BEAR Story

After I'd turned nineteen—the legal drinking age in Alabama at the time—I went to an alumni party sponsored by the Mobile Chapter. It had just tons of seafood—shrimp, oysters, crab claws, everything. There were a number of players there, and we were all having a pretty good time.

Coach Bryant came over to us as we were finishing some shots of tequila. "What is that, boys?" he asked.

"Tequila, sir," we responded, not knowing what he was going to do.

"Stay right here," he drawled. "I'll get you some tequila."

A moment later he came back with a mezcal bottle—worm and all—and handed it over.

"Take a shot of this," Coach Bryant offered.

I did. It set me afire all the way down.

"Tennessee tranquilizer," Bryant mumbled as he walked away.

Mezcal, tequila, moonshine—something *serious* was in that bottle.

The underlying lessons Coach Bryant taught are as varied as the individuals who learned them.

What I, Barry Krauss, learned is that big plays can change everything.

Now, every day of my life, I think about making big plays. What did I do that day? Did I make the play? It could be only an extra moment with my son in the car. That's a big play. A big moment. Was I there for my children? How did I do in the game of life today?

Should I make this deal, or will it compromise my principles? Did I do everything I could to win?

Every day I want to be able to say that I did my best.

Yes, Coach Bryant is still my coach.

5

The Usual Suspects in an Unusual Place

Fall, SEC Football, and the University of Alabama

The players in the movie *Field of Dreams* thought Iowa was heaven. They had obviously never been in our neck of the woods on a Saturday in the fall. Nothing short of a ride in the space shuttle can compare.

This grandiose celebration of life and football is something all of us in the SEC shared. It is highlighted in many ways but none better than the great story of a University of Georgia graduate invited to the yearly season-ending Texas-Oklahoma game at the fairgrounds in Dallas during the Texas State Fair. After taking part in all of the parties, the pomp, the picnics, and pregame festivities, the man's host looked at him just prior to kickoff, slapped him on the back and asked him wistfully, "Have you ever, in all your born days, seen anything like this hullabaloo?"

"Every Saturday in the SEC," the Georgia alumnus replied.

As great as the SEC is in comparison to the rest of the unison-chanting, card-flipping, body-painting, shaker-shaking, yelling-for-no-reason rest of the country— *Alabama is that far above the SEC.*

Yes, in the 1970s the university in Tuscaloosa that the Union cavalry burned to the ground in the 1860s was a whole other world—a world of its own—with unique culture, norms, mores, and standards. A better world. It was almost unreal—like Peter Pan's Never Never Land.

If, like Peter, you let it, it could be a wonderfully mystical land.

Alumni have told me it has always been this way. And it always will.

It is the mama that called Bear Bryant home. He loved her . . . as did Dr. Timothy Leary, Mr. Elvis Presley, and thousands of others. She welcomes us all back—just like we never left—while never telling our secrets. Like an old heartthrob she is our late date sneaking into our fraternity house. She is our 2:00 a.m. paramour and our best girl rolled into one. She is all of our college experiences.

It is BamaLand . . . a wonderful, almost imaginary place.

Don't get me wrong. BamaLand isn't just about football; it is an all-encompassing— engrossing—aura. It surrounds and engulfs all life. It invades your pores and infiltrates your very being.

Life is easy in BamaLand. Life is good in BamaLand. Just ask the alumni. They might tell you—if they don't mind your knowing the truth. So keep in mind this was our foundation, as well as the environment that fostered our actions, lives, and dreams.

BamaLand, 1975–1978

The moment I set foot on the hallowed ground of the University of Alabama, I knew this place was special. I had always been different, always just a little uncomfortable. Once there, I could be myself in spite of myself. I let down my guard and my hair—and I had a lot of it back then, just like everyone else.

What made BamaLand special was its characters. All types of characters. Characters with hats, characters who were rats, characters who prayed, characters who laid. It was a beautiful place.

It wasn't just a sex comedy. It was a serious place for fun education. And a fun place for serious education.

BamaLand.

For me, as a football player, life in BamaLand revolved around its king, Paul William "Bear" Bryant. Not only did he rule the kingdom; he ruled our lives.

Our football lives, however, were altogether too real—and painful. No Never Never Land for us.

Football players in the mid-1970s were a much-loved and much-hated group. Everyone respected what we did, but many didn't like the high value at which we were perceived. Jocks were a necessary evil. On a par with $75-a-barrel oil—you have to have it, but you feel justified at bitching about it, too.

Perhaps that ambiguity toward us made us crazy or put additional pressure on us to perform. I'm not a clinical psychologist, but I would guess that our "wild-assedness," as a group, had something to do with these contradictory demands.

And we were certainly "wild-assed."

The Usual Suspects

This is a great country, the United States of America. You are always innocent until proven guilty. Something like that. But, my point here is, even though I am calling this section "The Usual Suspects," we are all innocent.

This is the group of individuals that, if any crime had ever been perpetrated, would have kept me company in the police lineup. These are the guys I knew were always with me. Many of them I hung around with most of the time.

Later I will discuss some of the "usual shenanigans" in which I could have possibly been involved on any given day, from painting a cow to plowing a waist-high cornfield—at midnight—with Louis Green's car.

Uh, oh, I think I may have erred here. In an effort to allow these guys to maintain the credibility and respectability they have built over the past decades, and so diligently protect today, I will enact Barry's Law from this moment on for this book: never tie a shenanigan directly to a suspect. The exceptions will, of course, be really depraved actions for which no punishment or humiliation could be too harsh, and stupid stuff I elect to tell on myself. However, if a reader really concentrates, he or she can learn the identities of the suspects.

Sorry, Lou, I'll try to keep you clean from now on, if I can.

Below are listed just some of "the usual suspects." These are the guys who cannot deny their association with me. They were a key part of my life. Others, who could possibly be in positions of responsibility today, I have spared through omission from this section.

You guys know who you are. You owe me one. Or maybe more.

One of my best friends at Alabama was somewhat of a rival at home in Florida, Marty Lyons. Marty was from St. Petersburg Catholic High, and I first got to know him at a high school all-star game. We played against each other, and although we didn't form a bond there, we did respect one another. Hell, he was 6'5" and close to 280 pounds. I had to respect him.

Yet, when we hit Alabama, we became fast friends—in every sense of those words.

Through someone's infinite wisdom, Marty and I were tagged as roommates. Although I never really figured that one out, I'm sure it had something to do with us wearing each other out at about the same time, hence sparing the serious students and players who had to live with us in Bryant Hall from our shenanigans. Too bad we didn't spare Jack Rutledge, our coach who lived in the dorm, or his wife. More on that later.

Of all the Usual Suspects, Marty probably got in less trouble than anyone. Hell, I know why! He always blamed me for everything—which would be pretty close to the truth. Maybe it wasn't so much that Marty always landed on his feet as it was that he landed on me.

We have always had a great, complementary relationship.

Marty's other dominant characteristic was that he was always "in the know." No matter what, Marty knew what was going on! As I related earlier, that Sunday after I missed Coach Bryant's bed check, Marty was one of the first to console me.

"I wouldn't want to be you!" he said.

Lou Green's Side-BEAR Story

Coach Bryant didn't particularly care for all of the NCAA regulations that were being handed down in the fall of 1975—regulations restricting travel squads, home squads, scholarship limits, and stipulations on practices. They all got a lot of press and made it appear that football coaches were not really in charge of their own teams.

One day during the "meat" of practice, the offensive line was dragging. It happened to all of us at some time or another, but this day was their turn. We had all already been on the field for two hours—a scorching two hours.

Coach Bryant was up in the tower, seemingly halfway to heaven—and removed from the 110-degree temperature on the Astroturf—but fuming like the Devil. He came stomping down the tower ladder, strode out onto the turf, and into the offensive huddle. As you may have heard—Coach Bryant depended tremendously on his assistant coaches . . . his disciples. They ran practice; they were his word brought down to Earth. When he popped into the huddle, no one could believe it. Eleven mouths fell open.

He had everyone's attention.

"The NCAA can tell me how many practices I can have, but they can't tell me how long to practice! Start over!" Coach Bryant growled.

They did, and we were on the field another two hours—until the offensive line was kicking everyone's ass. Desperation can also be a great motivator.

He told us all what was going on. It got so prevalent that we nicknamed him "AP/UPI."

There was no piece of information too inconsequential—even how practice was going to be broken up any given day. We always had periods in practice in which we worked on certain things, and generally only the coaches knew about these in advance. Marty would somehow find out and pass that information on to everyone: "Yeah, practice today is going to be drills for ten, fifteen, and twenty minutes, and then we'll do two 'no time' periods." The "no time drills" were pure hell . . . all-out nonstop blood-and-guts effort until you got it right.

Anyway, we welcomed knowing what the day was to hold, and Marty always knew. So after he gave us the update, we would sing the Marty Lyons song—to the tune of "Mickey Mouse."

"M-A-R-T-Y L-Y-O-N-S, Marty Lyons, AP! Marty Lyons, UPI!"
You get the drift. We were football players, not singers or songwriters.

Lou Green has already been introduced—inadvertently—prior to the implementation of Barry's Law. Lou was a blast, an offensive lineman. Hell, he was a downright offensive person!

Just kidding, Lou. But take note—Lou became a rugby coach; that's the right game for him—wild, rough, and lots of pushing. Lou was a truly independent soul prior to souls gaining independence.

We who truly came to know Lou are richly blessed. His love of life, his wry smile, and his quiet confidence were all his outward trademarks. Underneath boiled "the Joker," trying desperately, constantly to escape and rule his outward body.

In BamaLand "the Joker" got out a lot.

Since I have already spilled the beans on Lou earlier, I must complete the story. Lou had a wonderful old car. Its most impressive feature was a magical bumper, which never showed a dent or scratch. I know for a fact that the car could run fifty-five miles per hour in a field with corn or grass above the hood. It was like us, invincible.

Those were the wildest rides I've ever had, blindly dashing through fields at an outrageous speed, laughing so hard I was about to choke.

And there wasn't ever a scratch on the bumper.

The moment Walter Iooss Jr. snapped the *Sports Illustrated* cover photo of me frozen at the top of my leap—head to head with Mike Guman—was indicative of my life at Alabama. I had completely lost all sensation on one side from the initial impact. It seemed like we were up there forever, and just when I feared some Nittany Lion was going to arrive in midair and push us over the goal line, Murray Legg came flying in from behind me and to my left to seal the deal.

Saved again.

It was indicative because that circumstance had been my life at Alabama—always on the edge. From bed check to first-round draft choice—life was always in the balance. And somebody, something, always picked me up—made me better and supported me as a front man.

This is where I tell you that I'm not stupid enough to believe those circumstances were always due to my teammates—I know for sure that the "Big Guy Upstairs" was responsible for most of it, through my teammates. Talk about working in mysterious ways.

Murray Legg was one of those good men who formed the backbone of our team, truly giving us the foundation, the faith, and the knowledge that a higher being was ultimately in charge—therefore releasing us to play our best for his glory and Alabama.

Flying-nail tough and dangerous, Murray showed his determination in the last two minutes of the Sugar Bowl as Penn State was trying desperately to come back. Penn State quarterback Chuck Fusina isolated Scott Fitzkee—their best receiver—on Murray long and down the middle. Murray didn't get beat on the play—the ball sailed over both their heads—but he got tangled up with the receiver. It could have gone either way—pass interference on either Legg or Fitzkee—but it was a good no-call. The entanglement turned a lot of heads. In some games it would have gathered a "makeup" call from stupid officials. Several plays later—on Penn State's fourth down from around the forty—Murray played "balls to the wall" aggressively, breaking up the pass and almost intercepting it to put them away. That, my friends, is confidence and grace under pressure. That was Murray.

Barry's Side-BEAR Story

Under normal circumstances—when we weren't playing LSU in Baton Rouge or Notre Dame in South Bend—one of Coach Bryant's beliefs was that if we dominated early, we would take the officials out of the game. It was a stated goal on many occasions.

In other words, beat your man early and often. Dominate him, and there would be less likelihood that a bad call could hurt us later.

That goal was still in effect in Baton Rouge, but it was secondary to the goal of taking the crowd out of the game. When in Baton Rouge, beat the crowd first, then kick LSU's ass. During my tenure it worked every time. But practicing under the loudspeakers simulating frantic LSU crowd noise was really a drag.

Paul Crane, Linebacker Coach Extraordinaire, was another of the "usual suspects." But Paul, like Murray, was always there to help balance out everything else in life. He was a favorite of all the players—laid back, a leader, and he wore a Super Bowl Ring from the World Champion New York Jets. Coach Crane had been a hero on Coach Bryant's great teams from the mid-1960s. All-American and All-SEC for Bama. We knew that he knew what it was all about, so we listened.

Lou Green shows off his invincible car, "Tank." (Courtesy of Lou Green)

And if tweaked perfectly, Paul Crane might even let you get by with a minor infraction of Coach Bryant's rules.

Paul made a career decision during my years at Alabama that looked to be a good move—but precluded him from taking over as head coach after Coach Bryant died.

"Steve Sloan had had some success at Vanderbilt and Texas Tech," Paul explains. "When he took the Head Coach job at Ole Miss, he offered me a position on his staff. I felt it was going to be a great stepping stone to the future.

"Before I took the job, Coach Bryant told me it was a bad decision," says Paul Crane today.

Paul went to Ole Miss under Steve Sloan. Sloan eventually lost control of the program, and everyone who had followed him there was set adrift.

"Coach Bryant was a fiercely loyal man," Paul continues. "He liked me and he believed in me. Years later, when I was considering a money management position, Coach Bryant offered to place half of all of his investments with me if that was what I wanted to do."

Barry proudly displays the ball he picked off on USC's two-point conversion try. His interception sealed Alabama's 21-20 win at the Los Angeles Coliseum on October 8, 1977. (Courtesy of Aaron O. Tesney)

Fellow middle linebacker Rich Wingo (36) shares a moment with Barry while the offense works its magic. At this time they had no inclination of the famous play that awaited them in New Orleans on January 1, 1979.

If Paul Crane had stayed at Alabama, there is an excellent chance he would have succeeded Coach Bryant; instead, Ray Perkins was brought in from the pro ranks. Who knows? If the cards had fallen into place, Paul Crane could still be the head coach of the Alabama Crimson Tide.

6

The Usual Shenanigans

As I mentioned earlier, the "usual suspects" in a number of incidents could have included anyone I knew in BamaLand—and they're all still innocent.

Therefore, no one will ever know exactly who may have acted irrationally at some point in his college career, executing some of the usual shenanigans.

First, I must warn you that these aren't your run-of-the-mill shenanigans of your average major university. These are shenanigans of epic proportions.

Some are very simple in vision and execution but are, in fact, ingenious. Others were dramatically complicated.

Authorities have not yet ruled out the involvement of alcohol in any of these incidents. Remember, these were innocent times—the good old days.

A1A Florida Keys "Big Guy" Diving Contest

Ahhhh, yes! Soon to be an Olympic sport, I'm sure. It all started on a well-planned spring break—six guys, one unbreakable car, four toothbrushes, and probably less than $50 apiece.

Through another of God's mysterious ways, we made it substantially unimpaired down into the Florida Keys, halfway to Key West, when we decided to stop for the evening on one of the islands. At the time, this particular stretch of old highway A1A contained both an old wooden-frame bridge and the new concrete one. Demanding tourists that we were, with no Hilton or Ritz available, we decided to sleep on the beach. Since it was still cold, we broke our firewood off the old bridge and we were home.

The following morning while our gang of hillbillies was taking "swim-baths," one of our larger suspects was dared to jump from the bridge.

"Not a problem," he said.

I couldn't believe he would do it, so I followed him up the bridge to the top. We were eighty or ninety feet up when he climbed up on the railing. No! Surely he wouldn't.

"If I crash, you guys pull me out, OK?"

"OK." "Sure." "You're kidding." Everyone swore he would be there.

Our large hero turned backward, immediately sprang into the air and began a back flip to the water nearly one hundred feet down. Sixteen feet per second, that's how fast you fall. Two-and-a-half seconds in the air . . . and he still didn't make it all the way around. He hit the water at an angle, and I immediately knew he was hurt.

Unconscious for only a moment, he came to the surface yelled for help. The two loyal friends who said they'd pull him out strolled up the beach to watch.

With mouth bloodied, two chipped front teeth, and a severely bruised leg, the diver finally made it out of the water.

"What the hell?" he said looking to his supposed rescuers.

"You did this to yourself, man. We couldn't get you out anyway; you're too damn big!"

Sometime later, standing on a pool table, the victim once again re-enacted the event—to the same end. But without the water this time. Lessons in diving, as in life, are sometimes learned the hard way.

An Exercise in Teamwork, Trust, and Crisis Negotiation

When all else fails, you could depend on your teammates. That is primarily due to the love, trust, and dependence you built on the practice field. And, of course, all of the planned exercises in teamwork, trust, and crisis negotiation you and your teammates have undergone.

So, you see, everything we did at Alabama had a reason.

That was the mind-set of a half-dozen of the "usual suspects" the night they decided to streak Tutwiler Hall—the seventeen-story female dorm just off Alabama's Sorority Row.

Two in the drop car, two in the pickup car, and two "in the buff," outfitted with the latest in ski masks and running shoes. The plan was perfectly timed: the drop car would pull up at Tutwiler and drop the runners off; they would then streak the east side of the dorm and dash through the parking lot to the back street, and the getaway car would already be there waiting. Perfectly planned. What could go wrong?

Everything!

The drop-off and dash went well. However, one streaker out-sprinted the other, and a pickup truck, seeing the fun, pulled up literally on the second's ass—horn blowing and lights blinking. By now, there are thirty yards between the two streakers, and the second guy, the trailing back on the play, knows he'll have to veer off on his own or implicate the whole crew to the growing audience.

The plan goes terribly wrong here.

Our second man cuts left, jumps a fence—still running full speed—then jumps another and tries to clear a couch that had just shown up in the open field to make the tackle. Bam, our man hits the ground. An elderly couple sit on their back porch, taking it all in, amazed.

"There goes a naked boy," the wife muses.

Meanwhile the leader hits the getaway car, long hair still flying from under his mask, and dives in the open door. The pickup truck is trying to navigate through the parking lot to identify the group.

"Where's so-and-so?" the driver queries.

"Who cares, go! Go! Go! Go!" the lead runner demands.

Tires spin and smoke rises as the successful getaway is completed—minus one-half of the cargo.

Meanwhile, back on the dark streets behind Tutwiler Hall a man walks a dog. From out of the shadows comes another man—naked from shoes to ski-mask—who approaches the dog walker. As a show of good faith the streaker pulls off the mask.

"Buddy, can you help me?" the streaker inquires.

"What do you need?"

"Your shirt, your pants, anything."

"Why?"

"I'm naked!" the streaker responds incredulously.

The now-familiar pickup truck engine can be heard racing down the side street, hunting its prey. At that moment the getaway car eases to the curb, and the door opens.

"Thanks a lot, buddy," the still naked streaker calls to the still-surprised man (and his dog) as he climbs into the car.

Coach would have been proud. Of the couch.

1-800-GINSU4U

Ahhh, yes. The 1970s were a wonderful time, marked in our memories and history as the genesis of the television direct-sale age. Nothing to pay now; cash-on-delivery would get you a Pocket-Fisherman, a Fry-Baby, or, our personal favorite, a full set of Ginsu knives.

One day, Marty Lyons walked into Bryant Hall from class to find a package waiting downstairs—his first set of Ginsu knives. "First set" would be the operative phrase here.

He subsequently collected almost every item advertised on television—all on a COD basis, of course—and all of which he never ordered.

Welcome to the A-Club
(Now why is this a good thing, again?)

There are an endless number of proud moments in a football player's life at the University of Alabama: your first varsity play; your first big hit on an opponent; a breakaway run; or your first great game. A-Club initiation is another of those milestones. It's fraternity initiation for those whose fraternity is the football team, a nation unto itself.

The new kids are gathered up—virtually naked—wearing only jocks, straw hats, and running shoes. They are unceremoniously—or in some cases ceremoniously—dumped somewhere, with the admonition that they should get back to Bryant Hall undetected.

Our group was dumped at Lake Tuscaloosa. Do you know how far that is from Bryant Hall? It's across a substantial river and up a long creek (or an even longer paved road, if you take that route). And the other killer—the only way back is over the Black Warrior River bridge on Alabama Highway 82. The bridge has a lot of helpful lights along it.

Run, hide. Hide, run. It's a pretty simple process, just take cover when cars go by—until you get to that bridge. Then, it's run like hell to get over it. It was quite a distance, not easy for a linebacker.

Well, it just so happened that as the first group of five was dashing over, along came a police car. The same thing with the second group. We were all given a ride back to Bryant Hall—no questions asked.

Many years later, knowing now what I didn't know then, I see Coach Bryant's helping hand in this rescue.

Good Morning, Mrs. Rutledge!
(AKA, "Barry, why are you here?")

Jack Rutledge had the hardest job of all the coaches on staff—he was the dorm coach and had to live downstairs with his family to keep an eye on us. He was sharp. He would go up on the roof with his binoculars and know everything that was happening on campus.

Of course, he had to go to bed sometime.

As freshmen, Marty and I were roommates on the second floor of Bryant Hall, just above the living quarters of Jack and his wife.

Like a lot of boys, we spent a good deal of time out of the dorm—you know, library, study hall, the bars—and sometimes didn't get back until late. On some occasions our arrival was less than quiet.

After an entire semester of these events, Jack Rutledge had had enough. One night after we came home in our usual fashion, there was a knock at the door. Jack took my arm and said, "Come with me for a minute."

We went downstairs and into the coach's living quarters . . . and then into his bedroom.

"Stay here!" he ordered.

About thirty seconds later an immense commotion breaks out just above my head.

At this point Mrs. Rutledge awakens, sits up in bed and squints at the 6'3"—245-pound figure standing at her bedside.

"Barry, what are you doing here?" she asked, calm and unaffected.

The noise from above continues, even louder, then stops.

"I think Coach Rutledge is trying to make a point," I finally said, embarrassed.

She turned over and immediately went back to sleep.

The next year, Lyons and I were separated. Marty landed on his feet again . . . He got a huge suite on the third floor, not even remotely close to Coach Rutledge's quarters. I'm sure I was the one who had started all the ruckus.

Can I Get You Something to Eat with That Volleyball?

Bryant Hall was a place of many happy times, wonderful friends, and learning about football.

The fact that it sat on "new" Fraternity Row was at times a problem. In fact, there was a fraternity house right behind us, with which we shared a parking lot. Now I'm not sure exactly how these young men came to believe that they had reserved parking rights in that lot, but it seemed that they certainly had that illusion.

They would always write nasty and impolite notes, stick them on our cars in the lot, and of course never sign them. Well one day there was a particularly foul note on one car that was picked up by a player on his way to class. He read it in class and just fumed richly.

When he got back late that afternoon, he pulled into the parking lot and noticed that virtually the whole fraternity was outside their house playing volleyball in the yard.

With no regard whatsoever for the score or the service, he pulled directly up onto the volleyball court, got out of his car, and held up the note.

In front of the whole fraternity he quizzed them. "Which one of you guys wrote this note? Come on fellas, you can tell me."

After much cajoling, however, no one owned up to it, and he finally gave up. But that ended the nasty note episodes. And probably had volleyball players easily distracted for a long time thereafter.

Rock and Roll, Baby!

College, for an athlete, is a wonderful experience. Yet with training, strict schedules, curfews, and coaches watching you like a hawk, the college experience is sometimes not what it could be. At one particular time, when we all had to be in the dorm, several of the usual suspects were standing by the windows watching a great party at the Sigma Alpha Epsilon fraternity house, just west of Bryant Hall. This was a kicking outside party: the yard was decorated, the band was great, and a whole bunch of good-looking girls were wandering around, seemingly untended. The crowd was so large that the yard had been fenced off, and they had even brought in porta-potties—and placed them a little too close to one of our cars.

We were watching this one guy with a particularly cute date. He was being a jerk to her and to a bunch of pledges. We couldn't believe a Bama man could get away with this kind of behavior.

Well, he made a mistake and went into the porta-john. We dashed downstairs, rushed over to the john and knocked it over. We rolled that thing halfway down their parking lot as the occupant screamed and yelled, thrashing around in its widely distributed contents.

Once the container had been properly shaken, not stirred, we made a hasty retreat to the dorm.

Are You That Hungry for a Krystal?

It's open all night, has cheap food, is just down the street, and—perhaps more important than everything else—you never know what you're going to see there at any moment past midnight. Krystal hamburgers. As I write this, there is a story in the *Tuscaloosa News* about a guy who has eaten five million Krystal hamburgers (they're kind of small) over twenty-nine years. They've got a picture of him smiling. So you understand the appeal.

Anyway, two of us were standing in line when one of our teammates sauntered in and took his place at the back of the line. We exchanged pleasantries and engaged in polite conversation while in line. Ten minutes later, after we had eaten in our car, he got his food and headed to the parking lot . . . still naked down to his shoes and covered in shaving cream.

Looking back on our escapades, I think I see a theme emerging. All I can say, it gets kind of hot in Tuscaloosa.

Hey, Let's Make a "Car Angel"

"Bluto" Blutarsky, in the movie *Animal House,* called on his fraternity brothers to participate in a totally senseless act. "We're just the ones to do it!" he said. Correct. It seems to have happened a lot back then.

One day, again on the way home from class I'm sure, someone noticed that a very nice car was parked right under a big retaining wall. Did I mention this was a nice car? And a big car? It was.

This guy climbed up that retaining wall, took a big jump and landed flat on his back on the roof of this nice, big car.

If you looked at it just right from above, you could almost see the figure of a 6'5" car angel.

Catching Anything?

Spring break outings were always fun in the 1970s. They were not like today's breaks—with thousands of kids and millions of MTV disk jockeys. And lots of police. You were pretty much on your own back then, with your own group. "Left to our own devices and imagination" would be an apt description.

The good times spiraled out of control once on the wharf in Destin, Florida. In dire need of a practical joke, we put our heads together.

Considering what was there, a shark hanging on display on the pier and a recreational vehicle parked close by, we formulated a plan to put the shark on top of the RV. It would be days before it really got gross.

It was working out pretty well at first; one of us was on top of the RV and two others were hoisting the shark upward when the family came out of a nearby restaurant. The mother was particularly mad. "Get off our car you drunken bums!"

The father, grinning broadly, watched from the back of the family as Mom shamed us off the RV and out of the parking lot.

Fifty Ways to Leave Your Local Bar

On a Thursday night just before the Tennessee game there must have been fifty football players at a bar on the wrong side of the tracks—Bahnhof's. It was a little hole-in-the-wall place with one front door and one back door, which led to an enclosed patio—with walls about eight feet tall.

That night Jack Rutledge, the dorm coach, had obviously caught on. Someone saw him walking toward the front door from the parking lot. Word made it inside like electricity.

Imagine a bar full of probably two hundred folks—and fifty of those dashing for the back door and climbing that eight-foot fence. Probably forty-three of us ran all the way to Bryant Hall, about four miles or so. The other seven were probably linemen.

The Junior Senator from California

Spring break! What a wonderful concept. Take all of your depravity to a totally new location, surrounded by totally new people—who didn't know you—and execute it to the best of your ability.

Well, maybe it wasn't actually that bad. Spring break did bring about great opportunities. But competition was everywhere . . . on the beach, in the bars, in the restaurants.

The place is Fort Walton Beach, Florida, around 1978. This once-peaceful community has done a great job of becoming a spring break mecca. Too good. The crowds on this trip are worse than ever—horrendous. It is Friday night and every restaurant in town has a two-hour wait. Major bummer. But not if you are creative.

Four extremely hungry guys have just completed a lap around town looking for the shortest lines. There are none.

Thinking quickly, they approach one of the young ladies they have met earlier on the beach—perhaps the only female within miles without a southern accent—and solicit her cooperation in their plan.

Cathy agrees and makes the telephone call.

"The junior senator from California is in town, studying and researching this region's success in tourism, and would like to see your operation and meet and talk with the manager and staff of the restaurant."

"We're covered up," was the harried response from the hostess.

"That's OK," Cathy responded. "We'll just watch you guys work and talk whenever you can."

"Let me talk to my manager," the hostess said as she put the phone down.

Three minutes later a man on the other end of the line inquires as what will be required from his people and how many will be in the party.

They had bought it!

We all dressed as respectably as possible and assigned the most mature-looking guy in the group (he had long hair and a beard) to be "the senator." With Cathy, our "chief of staff," leading the way, we loaded up the car and planned our actions on the way. At the restaurant she was great. She got us into the bar immediately, introduced "the senator" to the manager, and led the conversations with each of the servers and bartenders waiting on us.

Within minutes we were drinking free. In another ten minutes we had our food—at the bar where no one else was allowed to eat.

This went on for a couple of hours, with all pitchers on-the-house for the senator and his staff. Finally, one of our friends who wasn't in on the deal—and now extremely pissed that he wasn't receiving this same treatment—began to spill the beans on us.

We quickly had one of our "security people" escort him from the establishment, paid the food bill, and beat a path to our car—laughing all the way.

I am sure that someday I'll be watching the news and see Cathy sworn in as the junior senator from some western state. She'll be ready.

The Smart Car

The worst part of college was the walk across campus to get to class. It was always the same: wondering what we had missed when we slept through it last week, when we were going to have a test, or talking about who was going to be our date for homecoming.

Several of us had a night class together, which required this trek every Tuesday and Thursday. Week after week we would pass the same VW, in the same parking place by the library, with the keys in it. It was almost like its owner was daring us to play a joke on him.

One Tuesday night the campus seemed particularly desolate. Yet the VW was still there—with the keys dangling in the ignition.

It was too much for one of us to stand. He squeezed his 6′5″ frame into the VW as we watched in disbelief, then cranked the car. Yeoooow. He almost ran over us backing out and speeding down the street in reverse. We were frozen.

As he pulled onto the quad, we had to follow him to actually witness his evil plan. He stopped at the front of the library, put the car in low gear, and began to pull up the steps. We all broke into a run as the deed was just beginning.

As he put on the emergency brake on the Gorgas Library portico, the campus police pulled up to the back of the building, lights and sirens cutting through the night.

Being an athlete, the driver made his escape without capture after a long pursuit, although several of us may have been a bit late for class.

"It was still standing when we left, we promise"

Three of us decided to drop in on a really cool fraternity party—a Hell's Angels–theme party. There were motorcycles and old beat-up cars everywhere.

The fraternity members quickly recognized us and welcomed us into the party—free beer flowing freely, but no Tennessee Tranquilizer. After about an hour each of us got on a motorcycle. At first we were riding around the outside of the house—fun and cool. After a couple of more beers, we're riding around the inside of the house—including up the stairs, down the stairs, giving the fraternity brothers' dates rides.

You probably get the picture.

The fun lasted until very late, or maybe very early the following day, and we somehow wound up at home.

On Sunday morning I noticed—tremendously shocked—that the fraternity house had burned to the ground.

The three of us quickly got together and agreed that it was still standing when we left—we think.

Barry in his identity-confused quarterback days. (From the author's collection)

Linebacker, Pompano Beach High, 1974. (From the author's collection)

Mr. and Mrs. Krauss always enjoyed Alabama Football, seen here at the 1978 Homecoming game. (From the author's collection)

Coach Bryant and Barry, 1978.

Whether working or playing, this team stayed together. (From the author's collection)

"The Goal Line Stand." Barry makes the stop above the pile of humanity as Rich Wingo (36) takes on the lead man and Mike Clements (43) supports from the right. (Photo by Bernard Troncale, courtesy of the *Birmingham News*)

Barry, pictured here at the Meadowlands vs. the N.Y. Jets. (Photo by Donald Larson)

Barry and Marty Lyons renew the competitive fires again in 1988 as the Colts visited the Jets. (Photo by Donald Larson)

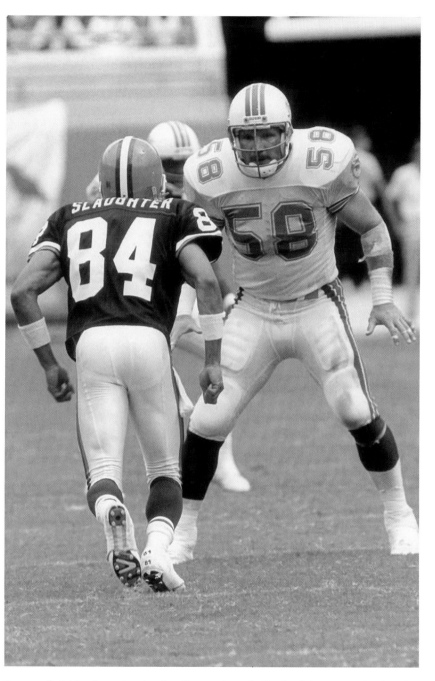

Even as a Dolphin, the road to the playoffs went through Cleveland. (Courtesy of Mike Julia)

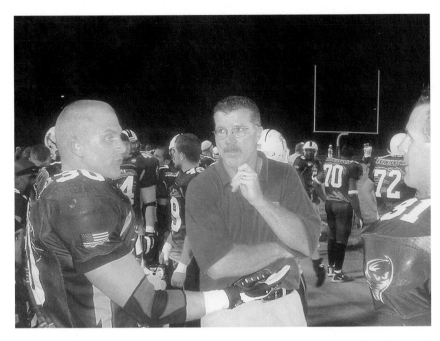

Barry and Doug Lavell discuss the strategy for Barry's Minor League team, the Indianapolis Tornados. (From the author's collection)

Coach Mike Shula shares a moment with Barry at a 2004 charity event. (Photo by Catherine Gurley Raulston)

The entire Bama Nation, including Joe Namath and Barry, look forward to occasional gatherings, like this benefit in Tuscaloosa in 2004. (Photo by Catherine Gurley Raulston)

Don Shula shares a moment with two of his Alabama pupils, Barry (left) and Bob Baumhower (right). (Photo by Catherine Gurley Raulston)

Kenny Stabler and Barry take a much needed break and relax after a tough radio show gig.

Barry and his wife Darcy. (Photo by Portrait Innovations)

Barry sits in front of his painting of the Goal Line Stand. The Digby Miller trophy, the Sugar Bowl MVP award, and a photograph of Coach Bryant surround the setting. Barry is the only defensive player to win the Digby Miller trophy from 1946 through the publication date of this book. (From the author's collection)

7

The 1978 Season

t seems almost crazy, but the 1978 season—that championship season—does not
tand out strongly in my mind at all. Actually I remember the individual games in
my sophomore year—the year I broke into the starting lineup—much better.

Perhaps I have blocked some memories of those 1978 games because of our
ess-than-tremendous start. We struggled in almost every game in the first half of
he season. We found ourselves behind in all of our first six games—including the
Vanderbilt game. More probably it is the fact that my compartmentalizing brain
has relegated all of those games to the status of mere stepping stones that brought
us to our "game of destiny." And that was what mattered most that year.

Coach Bryant, a still-burning Chesterfield in hand—Heaven, I'm sure, allows
he beloved earthly vices of those who were pure of heart and purpose—is this
moment looking down at me in disgust, knowing as he always did that I loved the
big game best, and preparing his speech for that last attitude adjustment—just prior
o letting me through those pearly gates: "Krauss, you better get straightened up!"

What I do remember well about that season—particularly in the first half, when
ve were always behind and slugging it out for every win—is that we were a Big Play
eam. We lived off of them. They turned losses into wins. They changed the momentum. They kept us alive.

Without a doubt the biggest play of the year was made by E. J. Junior in the
econd game of the season against Missouri. We had jumped out to a 17–0 lead
pretty handily by the middle of the second quarter. Then something happened. The
Tigers woke up and started kicking our butts. They had a long drive for a touchdown, shut us down on offense, a long run for another TD—and missed the PAT—
hen an interception return to score again. Within minutes our comfortable 17–0
ead had turned into a 20–17 deficit at halftime.

Coach Bryant was at his best in the locker room—or worst, depending on your
perspective. He chewed us out like never before.

It didn't do much, at least for the offense. We went out and had to immediately
punt our first possession of the second half. We were going nowhere fast. No, I take

that back. At that moment we were headed for Team Oblivion—the place where great teams without good breaks wind up—in 9-3 or 8-4 Hell.

E. J. Junior to the rescue. After holding Mizzou to three downs inside their own thirty-five yard line, E. J. flew in and blocked the punt, allowing Rickey Gilliland to scoop it up and run it in from about thirty yards out.

New game, new season, new confidence. It was the turning point of the year even though we would lose our next game against Southern Cal. We now knew we could come back. We thought we could beat anyone, anywhere. It was a big moment in a big game.

In a national championship season, every game is a big game. That year we opened the season with Nebraska in Birmingham. It doesn't get any bigger than this in college football: a nationally televised game on ABC—a huge event for us and the Huskers. And a huge risk.

The big games were always pretty easy for me to get up for, and Coach Bryant knew it. Yet he had to motivate everyone on the team—to their highest level—in order to get that perfect fever pitch. He would always have the coaches post clippings on the bulletin board of the attitudes and comments of our opponents. This year he had his own personal vendetta to use as inspiration.

The previous year we had played Nebraska in Lincoln—a clash of two traditional football powerhouses. Perhaps more important—a clash of two traditions. Just as we were going to halftime, someone in the Cornhusker crowd grabbed Coach Bryant's houndstooth hat. They began to pass it up into the stands, tossing it around like a beach ball at a rock concert. For them, I'm sure, it was pure fun. And then they beat us. For us, and for Coach Bryant, it was inspiration for the future.

Leading up to the opening game of 1978, the hat incident was heavy on Coach Bryant's mind. The loss, too. The coach didn't like to lose. There were multiple clippings of those hooligans, thugs, and ne'er-do-wells throwing that revered, almost sacred symbol of Alabama football upward toward the top of the stadium.

We beat them, 20-3, but we still had to depend on the big plays to do it. Don McNeal got a key interception and Rickey Gilliland got a fumble inside their three yard line.

Defensively, it was a great game. Nebraska never got inside of our thirty yard line.

Then, of course, came the Missouri game. After E. J. blocked the punt and Rickey ran it in, we shut them down. Our offense got cranked and put two more scores on the board. We thought we were on the way.

E. J. Junior tackles a USC running back as Barry and his teammates close in on the action.

BUMMER, BUMMER, BUMMER!

What do you get when you take a great running back—let's say, named Charles White—and build a team of big, athletic guys around him, then give them a great coach like John Robinson, who could inspire a cactus to live at the North Pole?

What you get is trouble for everyone who crosses their path.

That day was our turn. Coach Robinson had told his troops that this Alabama team was the best team he had seen since the 1972 USC team. He convinced them that it would take a monumental effort to beat us.

Well, he got that monumental effort. It wasn't just one thing that we did wrong or they did right. It was everything. They were quicker off the ball, bigger, stronger, and most important, seemed to want it more that day. It was extremely frustrating.

Yet we were always in the game. We felt we could win. Then late in the first half, as we were down 7-0, but were going in for a game-tying touchdown, we had a backbreaker call from one of the officials. Billy Jackson scored, according to one

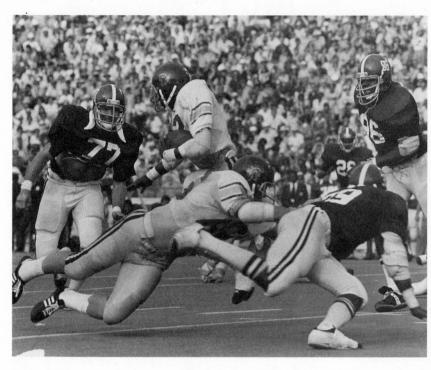

Barry closes for the kill on Charles White of USC, when Bama suffered their only loss in 1978.

official. That official was overruled by another, taking our six points off the board. Their defense firmed up and stopped us on two plays inside the one, giving them a tremendous goal line stand and slamming the door on our momentum.

Murray Legg got two fumbles, which helped keep us in the game.

But the death knell came when the sure-handed Don McNeal missed a perfect chance for an interception and tipped the ball to a USC receiver in the end zone for a TD. That scenario could come up nine million more times and McNeal catches every one of them. This wasn't our day.

They were good. We were nine for twenty passing, with four interceptions. That's not good.

More important, our kicking—not our kicking game, which included special teams—was horrendous. It was something that would continue to dog us through the first half of the season. We averaged thirty yards a punt, mostly from deep in our own territory. You can't give Charles White and USC that kind of field position and expect anything other than trouble.

Something happened to our team after the USC game. For some illogical reason an aura of confidence closed around us. We knew we could win in any situation. This newfound asset was both a blessing and a curse.

Of course, the curse part came first.

Vandy, always playing over their heads for us, was next.

You guessed it. We were down to them in the third quarter. At home! Yet we just knew we would break out of this funk.

Some in the crowd weren't as sure. For the first time in my life, our team was booed by our own crowd. It was a slap in the face and a wake-up call combined.

Once awakened, we scored thirty-five points in fourteen minutes.

The next week, you guessed it, we get down again—this time early—to the Washington Huskies in Seattle. Now, this comeback thing is getting a little monotonous. We need a new story line.

We tie the game, then give up a field goal. We're down again.

We need—all together now—a big play. E. J. Junior and Don McNeal brought a hard rush on the Husky punter, and he panicked and never got off the punt. He was tackled at the Husky sixteen, and it was the Tide's ball. Three plays later Tony Nathan scored. Then we missed another extra point!

They scored again, and had a chance to beat us late. Murray made an interception, which sealed the win, 20–17.

Next up, Florida, in Tuscaloosa. Different opponent, same story!

The Gators kicked an early field goal—and we're down 3–0. For six games in a row the mighty Crimson Tide has struggled from behind. One of those, USC, was a loss.

This was not Alabama football. Everyone knew it.

On the bright side, we managed to kick a couple of field goals. However, we punted the ball six times for an average of twenty-two yards, one a booming sixteen yarder, which could have hurt us except for . . . another big defensive play. We take a 23–12 win, but it wasn't pretty.

Going into the seventh game of the season—Tennessee, at Knoxville—we were not where we wanted to be. Sporting only one loss against some good teams, we were still pretty high in the polls for a team that had trailed in each of its games.

Tennessee was not the place to have questions answered. Even though we had won every meeting in my college career—and seven straight going into that 1978 meeting—Tennessee was like Auburn. All bets were off. Average teams would play

A big hit on the quarterback from Tennessee.

way over their heads, and better teams would press too hard and break down. College football.

We knew the place was fired up—almost literally, as the result of a riot the night before the game. Maybe that helped us focus. Maybe this was just the point where everything came together. In either case we were all happy about the victory.

Even more important, for the first time during the 1978 season, we played Alabama football!

We dominated on both sides of the ball. The offense scored thirty points by the end of the third quarter, with the second touchdown coming from a totally new offensive squad led by Steadman Shealey. That was a great sign.

On our side of the ball it was pure domination—until we got in our prevent defense. Although we gave up 341 yards, most of it in the fourth quarter when we got picked apart with short passes, we only gave up two TDs to win 30-17. This experience gave us some wisdom for a future date in the Superdome. We also got two fumbles and an interception.

Yes, this was Alabama football.

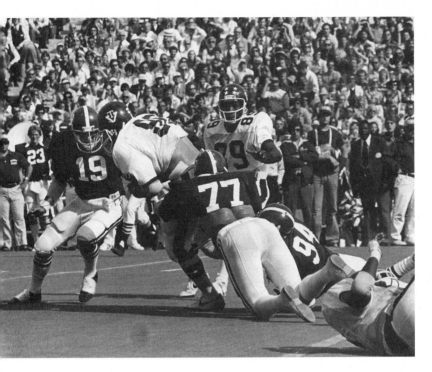

Barry, Wayne Hamilton, and Murray Legg drop a Virginia Tech runner at Homecoming 1978.

When Virginia Tech walked into Denny Stadium for our next game, they had to know the stars were aligned against them. They were catching us on our first real roll of the season, and at homecoming, no less.

It was our first shutout of the season, 35–0, but we still gave up 293 yards. Thank goodness the offense was on, with 444 yards split pretty evenly between the run and the pass.

More Alabama football. We even made *all* of our PATs.

Mississippi State came into Birmingham the following week seeing red, ready to play.

Unfortunately for them, once the game started most of the red they saw was ours—in their backfield. Our defense was at its best. The offense was good, too. We had them down 21–0 in the second quarter. At that point they resorted to a shotgun offense to try to elude our rush. They did have some success but not much.

It's hard for me to say with a straight face, but this was a defensive extravaganza. Don't laugh yet. Yes, we did give up 440 total yards. But we held them to minus sixteen yards rushing. We rushed the passer—even from his seven-yard-deep shot gun position—very effectively. We—a defense that was saddled with a give-up-the pass reputation—got four interceptions and three fumbles. And we kept them to two touchdowns. Try to think of another time when an offense had 456 passing yards and scored only fourteen points.

More important, we got a lot of practice—fifty-three plays—at pass defense.

LSU in Birmingham was a great southern football event. Charles Alexander was every bit as good a runner as Charles White of USC. We were just praying that the results would be different.

LSU's fate may have been sealed before the game.

When we heard Nebraska had beaten Oklahoma—Oklahoma had been number one—we got even more fired up about this game. We were number three. Unfortunately, the game started out like USC, not Mississippi State.

LSU drove the ball down the field early for a 7–0 lead. They intercepted a pass and returned it the distance but were flagged and the ball came back to inside their twenty. Another big play for us.

The offense finally got on track and put twenty-four points on the board in the second and third quarters. We shut them out in the second half for a 31–10 win.

Put in the proper perspective, we held a great LSU team, with one of the best running backs in the country, to 365 yards and 10 points.

Alabama football!

The best, hardest-fought game of the year was Auburn.

They had great talent on offense; Joe Cribbs, James Brooks, and William Andrews were all terrific. Their defense was good, too. And their quarterback, Charlie Trotman, was tough as nails.

We took the lead in the first quarter on a pass from Jeff Rutledge to Bruce Bolton, covering thirty-three yards.

Auburn came back. After a successful fake field goal, Joe Cribbs picked up his first of two touchdowns for the day on a five-yard run. Tied, 7–7.

Bama moved down the field and Alan McElroy kicked a thirty-four-yard field goal to give us a 10–7 lead.

But trouble lurked.

After recovering a fumble, the Tigers drove it down our throats, and Cribbs again made us pay with a nine-yard run up the middle. They missed the PAT but had a 13–10 lead.

We went nowhere, and then it was their turn. The clock was running out on the first half. When our defense came back onto the field, we knew they thought they had us where they wanted us. They would run out the clock, protect their lead, and formulate new plans of attack at halftime.

Alleluia! Alleluia! William Andrews fumbled a clock-killer of a run, and we got it at the twenty. Rutledge found Bruce Bolton for a TD, and we added the PAT to take a 17–13 lead. The game turned around, and we kept it that way.

We dominated the second half . . . It was ours.

At the end of the game the statistics showed a runaway: 427 total yards for the good guys to 233 for the bad guys. Final score, 34–16. The stats lied. The Auburn game could have gone either way at any moment. They had the talent to exploit a break if we had faltered. Cribbs, Andrews, and Brooks were too much of a threat to ever hold mute for a full game.

We were lucky.

Hell, that game was exemplary of our entire season. Hang on, hang on, get a break, come back.

When we walked off the Legion Field turf that day, we had earned a Sugar Bowl berth as the number two team in the nation, playing the number one team, Penn State.

Where was USC?

USC had lost to Arizona State on October 14, in Tempe. So USC was off to the Rose Bowl, where they would beat a fine Michigan team, 17–10.

We were off to face a Penn State team that was 11–0, and they didn't care about USC or Arizona State. They were ranked number one in the country, and all they had to do to confirm it was to beat an Alabama team that some said was more lucky than good.

The Chance of a Lifetime.

8

The Goal Line Stand

An errant pitchout bounced off the running back and was recovered by Penn State at the Alabama nineteen yard line.

On their first play Penn State's Matt Suhey picked up eleven yards to the eight yard line. He was stopped by Jim Bob Harris and Murray Legg.

It was first and goal. Mike Guman picked up two to the six yard line, where Rickey Gilliland stopped him cold. But Gilliland was injured with a pinched nerve and took himself out of the game.

Second down, goal-to-go at the six yard line. A wide receiver took cornerback Don McNeal deep in the end zone, and quarterback Chuck Fusina threw to Scott Fitzkee dashing toward the sideline. McNeal noticed Fusina's move, broke from his man and came up in time to miraculously wrangle Fitzkee out of bounds at the one yard line.

Third down from the one yard line. Guman led the way, blocking up the middle as Fusina gave the ball to Suhey. Krauss took Guman on at the line and jammed the blocker. Suhey leapt but met David Hannah on the way up and Rich Wingo at the top. The ball was spotted less than a foot from the goal line.

Fourth down, less than a foot to the goal line. Suhey led the way up the middle, Fusina handed the ball to Guman; a mirror image of the previous play. Wingo took on the blocker and stopped him cold, just like it has been drawn up in countless practices. The defensive linemen had established a new line of scrimmage. Guman leaped, as did Krauss. The two hit perfectly squarely and were suspended in midair, almost lifeless—Krauss was paralyzed on his left side, Guman was unconscious for a moment. Murray Legg sealed the pile from any forward movement, and Krauss and Guman went straight down—*outside* the Alabama end zone!

Those were the bare facts, the objective data: uninfluenced by emotion, surmise, or personal opinion.

The Alabama crowd, on the other hand, was extremely subjective: they screamed in delight, rocking the Superdome down to its foundation.

Subjectively, for Alabama fans, this was the greatest goal line stand in all of football. The fourth-down play has been named by ESPN as one of the top ten single plays in the history of college football, another subjective but well-founded opinion.

My teammates and I agree. Here is our story.

When I opened the heavy curtains on my New Orleans hotel window, the only thing I could see was the rain trickling down the thick glass and the dank, gray skies in the distance. This day, January 1, 1979, was the most important day any college football team could have. As I continued to stare out the window—looking through the condensation and drizzle—I noticed the throngs of fans braving the weather, dashing across the streets, and hurrying to claim their seat for this classic.

All we had to do now was play the game.

This game, like much of the 1978 season itself, is a blur. It was, however, crystal clear that defense would win the day. Throughout the first half the defenses, on both sides of the ball, had dominated. Our defense had taken the game to the guys in blue and white. If it had been a boxing match, we would have been ahead on points. It wasn't boxing. The score was tied 0–0 as halftime closed in on us. We got the ball at our own twenty with around 1:30 on the clock. We went up the middle twice—showing our willingness to run out the clock. Penn State called time-out twice—insinuating they planned to stop us here and have another shot at trying to put something on the board before halftime.

Then we got a first down, blowing their strategy. On the next play Tony Nathan's thirty-yard run blew the top off the dome. At the PSU thirty-seven Alabama had a chance to score and called time-out.

On the next play Jeff Rutledge hit Bruce Bolton on a thirty-seven-yard post pattern. Bruce was wide open and made a careful catch, cradling the ball with his body while falling into the end zone. Like lightning, we had a 7–0 lead going into halftime.

In the third quarter Penn State drew first blood. They picked off a Rutledge pass and returned it to just inside our territory at the forty-eight. A couple of plays later Scott Fitzkee took in a great pass from Fusina for a touchdown and a 7–7 tie.

Our "dominant defense" had just given up almost fifty yards in no time.

On the next Penn State series we managed to force a punt—which Lou Ikner returned thirty yards or so to around the ten yard line. We couldn't punch it in on two tries. On third down Jeff pitched to Major Ogilvie, who took it in to give us back our lead, 14–7.

We hammered each other back and forth until around the 8:00 minute mark in the fourth quarter.

That was when Penn State got the fumble.

"Running back on the field after the turnover," said Don McNeal, "I knew we could stop them. Our offense had covered for our mistakes all year; now it was our turn to pick up the pieces. We all knew we could stop them."

Don was absolutely right. To have any other perspective would have been to quit . . . and by now you know that thought didn't exist under any crimson helmet in the Dome that day.

Once we were on the field, there was no sense of panic but a huge feeling of urgency. We all held hands in the huddle and said we had to do it. We all knew it.

There was one other factor in our confidence: our preparation. We lived preparation.

Our secret weapon and defensive coordinator, Ken Donahue, was without a doubt the most well-prepared coach ever to stalk the sidelines for a major college. At that time Coach Donahue had already spent a lifetime watching film; I don't know where he found additional time for coaching, not to mention just living. He knew everything about every competitor we lined up against. Not just their tendencies to run certain plays in certain positions, every detail about them. How did the left tackle change his stance for a run? How many times did they run a quarterback sneak over left guard instead of right guard or center, and why?

Ken Donahue, personally, was responsible for picking up a key against Tennessee that was good for four years—and four victories in just the time I was there. The Tennessee center was Robert Shaw. He was a good center, a great blocker, and a leader for their team. However, he had a habit of doing something just a little differently on runs than he did on pass plays. Coach Donahue caught the fact that Shaw would set the ball just a little more out in front of him on a running play. That way he could snap the ball and fire out at the same time. For a pass he put the ball back a bit. He wanted to be able to stand erect quickly to pass block. This key, as infinitesimal as it was, worked for us for four years.

Another key Coach Donahue picked up was a lot more apparent. Ottis Anderson, a tremendous running back at the University of Miami, had a bad habit. Like all running backs, he would always get into a three-point stance. However, if Ottis was set to go to his right, he would have his left hand down. If he was going left, he would have his right hand down. When Coach picked it up, we couldn't believe it. It was so simple it was crazy. And why didn't other teams pick it up too? The only thing I could ever figure out was that he was probably ambidextrous and looked absolutely natural lining up either way. Therefore, no one noticed. Except Ken Donahue.

We put in a special shift for Ottis Anderson and the University of Miami, and boy, did they have a bad day.

Unfortunately, Penn State was an extremely well-coached team. There were no keys to read that gave anything away. This was an all-out, in your face, we-think-we're-better-than-you football game.

However, there was something Coach Donahue had done. In order to get more pressure on their All-America quarterback, Chuck Fusina, we had put in what he called a "slide defense." Today, it's called a delayed blitz, and it was pretty simple. Basically, the strong side linebacker—the one on the tight end side—would blitz whenever the quarterback rolled out to pass. They were trying to negate our pass rush with the roll out. When they did that, we had an extra linebacker in their backfield. That kept us in Fusina's face all day long.

The Sugar Bowl game was the hardest hitting, cleanest game in which we had played all year. That was the consensus from everyone in an Alabama uniform. And after the game, when pockets of Penn State and Alabama players got together on Bourbon Street, we learned they felt the same way.

So when we ran onto the field with the ball at the nineteen, we knew they would come directly at us. No trickery. They would have to execute the fundamentals better than we did in order to win.

"Our defense," said Rickey Gilliland, "pretty much was always looking for a three-and-out every time we ran on the field. From the nineteen, I felt that if we held them to a field goal we were the winner."

The Suhey run from the nineteen to the eight yard line was a staggering blow. All of a sudden it was here. First down inside the eight.

"The day before, in practice," said David Hannah, "we had walked through a goal line stand defense. All of us were saying, 'This is where it will happen; this will be the Gut Check.' And now, not twenty-four hours later, here we are."

Murray Legg was the first to verbalize it.

"Gut check! This is what we've always waited for! This is it!"

On the first play Matt Suhey bulled ahead until he was stopped cold by Rickey

Gilliland at the six yard line. Rickey knew he was hurt immediately, so he took himself out. Rich Wingo noticed him coming off the field and took it on himself to enter the game.

"When I saw Rickey was injured, I wasn't going to wait on some coach to make that decision," said Rich. "I just grabbed my helmet and sprinted onto the field."

"I didn't expect to play at all," Wingo continued. "Earlier in the season I had hit a fullback and his knee caught me in the back and herniated a disk in thirteen places. I didn't play in either the LSU or Auburn games. I just knew this would be my last football game, and I wanted to contribute."

On second down the defensive play by Don McNeal was the best play by a defensive back I have ever seen. Keith Jackson, of ABC Sports, sang Don's praises loudly on the air. Don had been taken deep into the end zone covering the wide receiver.

"Fitzkee was my man," says Murray Legg, "and my mistake. We had watched every Penn State game from the entire season on film, and, with only two exceptions, they dragged Scott Fitzkee across the field every time he lined up at tight end. I felt I knew just where he was going. I lined up inside of him and got ready, in my mind, to pick off the pass and go ninety-nine yards for the TD."

"Of course," continued Legg, "this was another exception. Fitzkee never even looked to the middle. He shot straight toward the sideline, paralleling the goal line. Since I'm inside, waiting on him, I'm already beat."

"Somehow out of the corner of my eye," said McNeal, "I saw Fusina throw the pass to the guy heading down the goal line toward the sideline. I just reacted."

Don beat the block of the wide receiver he had been covering, and flashed up to hit Fitzkee.

"'I can't let him fall one way or the other' was my first thought," remembers Don. "So I took him straight out of bounds—luckily at the one yard line. Curtiss McGriff, my roommate, picked me up, hugged me, and said, 'That's one heck of a play,'" McNeal recalled.

"It was all purely reaction," he continued, "from the hours and hours on the practice field. And Coach Donahue's preparation. We knew everything Penn State did, in every situation. We knew all of our assignments for any set they were in, and for any move they made."

Third down, the ball now inside the one.

Ken Donahue made the defensive call from the sideline. It would be a "pinch." Everyone would pinch inside—including the defensive backs inside the ends. The defensive ends would have pass coverage if a tight end broke out. The safety was "naked" in the middle, especially on a play action pass.

Byron Braggs remembered the moment perfectly.

"Heels in the end zone, get lower than your man, no margin for error," he clicked off the rules like The Ten Commandments. "Absolutely no margin for error, they couldn't gain an inch. Stalemate was no good," he continued. "It was too close. We had to establish a new line of scrimmage. And it was our place to free up the line-backers."

Is it any wonder Rich Wingo and I liked playing behind these guys? They were great!

"The Goal Line Stand was about getting lower than the offense and wanting it more," continued Byron. "We tried to get our hands inside, on the offensive line-men's legs, and push them back into the play."

"Their offense was built on the premise that their line should get a one-yard push by the time the quarterback turned. We couldn't afford that—we couldn't give up an inch."

"The first time I remember anyone calling 'Gut Check' was when the ball made the one yard line for third down," said Mike Clements. "It was Murray Legg. He was workmanlike serious, with a tinge of enthusiasm. But overall it was pretty calm. I don't remember anyone talking to anyone from Penn State, but of course I was on the opposite side from Marty."

"What I do remember," continued Mike, "is this: Every man, every player, had the look of supreme confidence in his eyes. We had watched every film, every play Penn State had run all year long. When the play was called, we had confidence."

David Hannah today sees himself as the luckiest player on the field.

"I played four plays that game—all of them in The Goal Line Stand," said Hannah. "The day before the game the team doctor drained one hundred ccs of fluid off my knee. I didn't know it but the coaches made the decision not to play me after that. I would never have been in if Warren Lyles hadn't pulled his hamstring."

"On the third-down play," Hannah continued, "I did an inside gap technique—lowering my left shoulder going right—and slid under the offensive lineman. I actually got a good hit on Suhey as he was trying to go up. I even got a hand on Guman on fourth down using the same move."

"The third-down play," said Rich Wingo, "where Guman led up the middle and Suhey tried to dive over, was the same play as the one on fourth down, except to the opposite side. Barry and I, the two middle linebackers, had the same responsibilities, according to where the ball went."

"On third," Wingo continued, "Barry had to get the first man, which he did, and I went up and stopped the diver."

After the third down the ball was marked less than a foot from the goal line after we all unpiled.

Chuck Fusina looked to the sideline, at the official, and then called time-out. He trotted over to discuss the situation with Coach Paterno and his assistants.

As it happened, this was expanded into a TV time-out, so the time dragged on forever.

He ran back on the field to take a good look at exactly how much real estate they would have to take for the touchdown—within feet of Marty Lyons.

"Fusina and I had been in New York earlier," said Marty Lyons of that moment, "for the 'Bob Hope All-Americans Celebration,' and we had gotten to know each other.

"He came up," Marty continues, "still looking, and said something like, 'What do you think?'

'You have to pass the ball,' I responded. It was all a very good-natured thing."

After inspecting the hash mark, Fusina went back to the sidelines and communicated again with Coach Paterno, surrounded by his assistants.

"I flashed back to a dream I had earlier in the week," said E. J. Junior, a defensive end. "In that dream we were on the goal line—just like now—and they came at me. It was an easy decision for them—I was the youngest, least experienced, and smallest. If I were them, I would have gone at me," Junior said, laughing. "I still would. Look at our guys—Wayne Hamilton, David Hannah, Curtiss McGriff, Byron Braggs, Marty Lyons, Barry Krauss, Rich Wingo—they were big, tough men. Yep, I just knew they were coming to me, so I was thinking about beating my man, no matter what."

"There was an absolute resolve in the huddle before fourth down," said Rich Wingo. "This was what, as a defensive player, you always dreamed about. The one who wanted it more was going to get it.

"I don't remember Marty saying anything," continued Wingo, "but of course I was on the other side of the line. We were really focused."

"Personally," said Mike Clements, "during the stand I was concentrating on staying focused. I knew there were at least two million people watching the game—watching us. There was so much going on it was almost hard to concentrate. And, to top it off, there was this television time-out—which just went on forever."

"I was just praying, 'Lord, help me do my job!'" said Don McNeal. "I didn't want to let my teammates down. I don't remember anything much about the crowd or the time or anything—I was just watching my keys, trying to figure out the formations and remember what my job was on each."

Once the time-out ended, Penn State was pretty quick to act. As soon as the official put the ball in play, they were moving.

A quick snap! Curtiss McGriff, Byron Braggs, David Hannah, Wayne Hamilton, Marty Lyons, and E. J. Junior all surged forward, pushing back one of the best offensive lines in history. Mike Clements and Don McNeal plugged the gaps inside the defensive ends. Wingo took the lead man, who had received the fake, head-on—also outside the end zone.

"We met helmet to helmet," Rich said. "I jammed him, but I didn't know if he had the ball. I knew that if he did, he didn't score."

Fusina gave the ball to Guman, who had to go up immediately.

Instinctively, I went up too. We crashed together perfectly square.

Time stopped!

We were suspended somewhere above the goal line on the Poydras Street side of the Superdome. Time—everywhere—stopped. Thinking back on it, it seems as if the whole world did a full revolution as nothing happened. It was raining outside. The bars in the French Quarter had folks watching in mid-sip of their beers.

It was deathly quiet. My left side was paralyzed; my helmet was broken.

Hurry, hurry, hurry! Somebody!

Sounds—screams and yells—started up again.

Hummmmphhhfff.

Murray Legg hit me from behind sealing off any potential progress Guman could make if assisted from his side. We crumpled down on to the pile.

The whistle blew . . . finally! It was over. I did not know the outcome, but, I was not alone.

"I pinched in on the play," said E. J. Junior. "My main responsibility was the quarterback or a pitchman, but I knew it was a run up the middle from the snap. From where I was, there was nothing I could do. I saw it all, though. Looking down that line there was no doubt Barry stopped him."

"I heard the crowd," said Wingo, "but in the pile I had no idea which side was cheering."

"I was pressed to the turf," said David Hannah. "The only thing I could move was my eyeballs. I didn't know which side was cheering. Penn State was wearing white socks and white tennis shoes. We were wearing black shoes, with white and red socks. As the pile was disassembling, I got a horrifying sight. I saw someone wearing white shoes jumping around. It was only after I got up and saw Marty Lyons—who had wrapped his shoes and socks in white tape—dancing up and down in glee, that I knew we had done it."

I was the last to know. Lying on the turf, still paralyzed, I saw Marty, who came to stand over me.

"We did it buddy," he said.

"We did it," I thought, feeling a little better already.

9

Reality Check

Looking back into my ever-receding memory, that frozen moment when I was face-to-face with Mike Guman at the top of that pile of humanity, suspended above the artificial turf of the Superdome, is one that is burned into my mind and my life. If there was ever one person whose life was totally changed by actions occurring in a single instant, I am that person.

That emotionally charged instant, that moment on live television, which was also captured on the cover of *Sports Illustrated* by photographer Walter Iooss Jr., burned me into the minds of thousands, or maybe even millions, of Americans. For better or for worse, I became a part of the lives of those who had been impacted by that play.

As a result, I was instantly accepted into every family within the universe of Alabama fans and instantly derided by those who were associated in any way with the blue and white of Penn State.

Football fans the world over appreciated my part in the pure drama of the play.

Almost without fail, whenever I meet someone new—no matter where in the United States—and they make the connection between Barry Krauss the man and Barry Krauss the football player, they associate me with that play. My twelve-year pro career never comes up.

"I know exactly where I was when you hit that Penn State guy," they might relate. "I was standing in the kitchen mixing a batch of onion dip. No sir, I'll never forget that."

It has happened thousands of times, in hundreds of places.

At this point I have to say I am flattered that anything I ever accomplished as a member of a team had so positively impacted a portion of the population. I assure you, my reader, that there were eleven men wearing crimson on the field that moment who could—*and would*—have made that play had it come to them. It had already happened: Gilliland on first down; McNeal on second down; Wingo on third.

At that instant, that frozen moment, I was only doing the job that had been taught me through thousands of drills in hundreds of practices throughout my Alabama career.

The most important fact of "The Goal Line Stand" is this: under that pile, on the sidelines, and in every home of every player who ever played for Alabama were the real people who made that play. Parents—who loved the traditions, the morals, and the ethics of Coach Paul "Bear" Bryant and the University of Alabama so much that they entrusted their children to the man and his system—made the play. Assistant coaches—who gave up real lives to teach us the game the way Coach Bryant knew was best—made the play. Our teammates on the sideline—who sweated out every practice with us, even though they may have never had the opportunity to wear the red or white practice jerseys of starters—made the play. And, most important, my fellow defenders on the field—each of whom believed in the system and did his job perfectly, leaving me only to do my job—made that play.

All of these people were at the top of that pile with me. I may have never verbalized it before this moment, but, because they were in Coach Bryant's system, they have always known it.

That is the reality of the event.

Thank you all.

As any player who ever played under Coach Bryant can tell you, what they all saw that day was only what Coach Bryant expected: every player doing his job.

He had taught us well.

Leaving Alabama, I took not just the results of one play but the lessons of a lifetime taught in four short years. Those are the lessons I still use every day. Thinking about it now, melancholy envelops me: I am afraid I took more than I gave, and it makes me sad.

Byron Braggs, who also played on the following year's undefeated national championship team, put it into words almost perfectly.

"As I was leaving Alabama," said Byron, "I had two thoughts: one, cry; and two, apologize. To say I'm sorry for the times I didn't give it everything, the stupid stuff I did, the times I didn't pay attention."

Byron learned Coach Bryant's lessons of life well. Once he had made the NFL, he went back to Coach Bryant and asked the question most of us never got around to asking.

"I asked him," Byron related, "what can I do to repay you, Coach?"

The response was true Bear Bryant.

"Just do something good for someone else," said the coach.

That was the reality of Coach Bryant.

10

The Vanquished

The Sugar Bowl of January 1, 1979, was much more than a football game. It was a clash of two of college football's dominant traditions, a personal battle between two of the greatest coaches to ever step on a field, and a football game that would mark participants and fans for life.

The gladiators in the middle of this royal competition, Paul "Bear" Bryant and Joe Paterno, put teams on the field that reflected their class, their dedication, and their will to win.

These two teams—if Paterno and Bryant had the ability to magically suspend time and play with only them throughout the decade—would have dominated college football in the 1970s. In my opinion these two would have been the top two ranked every year, and the national championship would have always come back to this head-to-head battle. (My apologies to my teammates on the 1979 team.)

Dropping the metaphors and imaginary scenarios, it was a hell of a game.

According to members of both teams, this game was played at a higher level than any other all year. The execution was better, the hitting was harder: it was a fabulous game. Speaking from Alabama's perspective, both teams played far above anyone on our schedule—including Southern Cal, Nebraska, Missouri, Washington, LSU, Tennessee, and Auburn. It was also a clean game on both sides. Doing a little celebrating in the French Quarter that night, Marty and I met up with several Penn State players. They were tremendously nice guys. They were sincere and forthright in saying we were the best team on the field that day. They also agreed that it was the toughest—but cleanest—game of their season.

"I passed and took some heavy licks," said Mike Clements, "and always had someone in blue and white sticking out a hand and saying, 'Good job 43,' as they helped me up."

These teams played with the class and dignity instilled by their leaders. It was a damn crying shame that either one of them had to lose.

Even though Penn State came up short on the scoreboard that day, they were not losers. They had won an important public-perception battle.

It was a battle Joe Paterno and Coach Bryant had been fighting for years, the battle for recognition of their programs as the perennially dominant. Both teams staked their place as legitimate football powers that day.

Other programs—Notre Dame is the perfect example—were held aloft by the national media as the paragons of college football. Although they had wonderful teams and great coaching, no one could ever cut through the media veil and see the real contents of the program. These favored teams were always being showcased by the national media, sportscasters, and the polls. Penn State and Alabama people—coaches, players, and fans—shared a common disdain for teams that took advantage of their "media-darling" position.

There was never any doubt that a 10-2 Notre Dame team, with a bowl win of any type, would jump over an 11-1, or even a 12-0, Alabama or Penn State team to steal the national championship. It had happened over and over.

Coaches Paterno and Bryant lived with this bias every day—and worked relentlessly to overcome it.

For Alabama the win and the resulting national championship put the program at the level it should have attained years previously. It also set the stage for a repeat championship in 1979, again culminating in New Orleans at the Sugar Bowl, this time with the Tide defeating Arkansas.

For Joe Paterno and Penn State the game reinforced their strength and their confidence. They were a dominant team, missing a national championship by only inches. Quite probably, it was the persuasion of Coach Paterno's assistant coaches that cost Penn State a national championship.

> I called a time-out and told my coaches I wanted quarterback Chuck Fusina to fake a run and throw a little pop pass to the tight end.
>
> A couple of my soundest coaches insisted I play the percentages—just crash through the couple of feet for the touchdown.
>
> "If we can't do this," the coaches argued, "we don't deserve a national championship."
>
> With an eerie clarity, I still remember the sure voice of my instinct: "That's a lot of crap. This is the time to surprise them and throw the football." (Joe Paterno in his 1989 autobiography, *Paterno: By the Book*)

Joe Paterno made the mistake of second-guessing himself at a very important moment. A pass might have scored—but, again, it might not have.

Instead, Penn State fans live with knowing they ran Coach Paterno's second choice of a play when they lost the national championship. And they rationalize the call.

When I first called Coach Paterno to request his cooperation for this project—twenty-five years after the event—the switchboard operator put me straight through to his assistant. She had the wonderful perky voice of a young woman, probably not more than twenty-five herself.

"My name is Barry Krauss and I am calling Coach Paterno to request his cooperation in a book project," I said trying to provide all the needed information without being long-winded.

"He made it!" she blurted loudly.

"I'm sorry?" I responded.

"He made it! Mike Guman scored."

We both broke into laughter.

Sometimes the fans take a loss harder than the players.

Guman knows the truth. Sort of.

"I didn't score; they made a great play. But I think Matt might have gotten in on third down," said Guman in a 2003 interview with *CentreDaily.com*, State College's home page.

Today, as I travel around the country on business, I am constantly regaled with this story or that about how The Goal Line Stand ruined Penn State or Joe Paterno. "Bunk!" I say to that.

That game, that play, was no more damaging to Joe Paterno or Penn State than a missed call by an official buried somewhere in an 8-4 season. Things might have been different if the play had worked out the other way, but there was no damage. Just the opposite was true. They were not beaten, just vanquished temporarily until they gained another chance to play and win it all on another day. Penn State, Joe Paterno, the players, and their fans all came off looking like the classiest football program in the United States. In my opinion, they were.

Coach Paterno also learned a lesson from that play. Eight years later he beat a good Alabama team on his way to the 1986 national championship. In virtually the same situation—with Alabama in a goal line stand situation—Paterno ran the play he wanted to run in the 1979 Sugar Bowl, according to senior Crimson Tide staff members. And Penn State scored. It was a little shallow pop pass just in the end zone. It was open because—just like in the Sugar Bowl—Alabama had gambled everything to stop the run. Paterno's team grabbed what was then a rare win in

Tuscaloosa to boost their status in their championship run. They won it all that year.

Of course that is little solace to those die-hard Penn State fans in the Dome that Sugar Bowl day or watching the game on television. However, Penn State fans always come off as good sports, as the following song parody proves. It is sung to the tune of Don McLean's "American Pie":

"The Day the Lion Cried"

A long, long time ago
I can still remember
How Fusina used to make me smile
And I knew that if they beat the clock
They would make New Orleans rock
And maybe we'd be happy for a while

Did you write the book of plays
And do you have faith in Joe Pa's ways
If the Lion tells you so
Now do you believe in Paterno
And can football save your mortal soul
And can you teach me how to play for Joe

Well I saw them standing at the hike
And I saw Chuck hand the ball to Mike
They all rushed to the hole (all rushed to the hole)
Man, I hate those fourth down and goals

I was a lonely teenage Penn State fan
With a blue carnation and a Chevy van
But I knew the game was out of hand
The day the Lion cried
I started crying

Bye bye National Championship
Drove my Chevy to New Orleans but the Tide won the trip
And good ol' boys were drinkin' whiskey and beer

Singin', "This will be the game of the year,
This will be the game of the year."

I met a girl who wore the blues
And I asked her for some happy news
But she just cried and turned away
Well I went down to the campus store
Where I'd heard the Blue Band months before
But the man there said the music wouldn't play

Well now in the streets the fans all screamed
[the fans all screamed]
The Lions cried and Bear Bryant beamed
[Bear Bryant beamed]
But not a word was spoken [not a word was spoken]
The vict'ry bell was broken

And the three men I admired the most
Paterno, Rip, and Higgin's Ghost
They caught the bus from the Gulf Coast
The day the Lion cried
We started crying

Bye bye National Championship
Drove my Chevy to New Orleans but the Tide won the trip
And good ol' boys were drinkin' whiskey and beer
Singin', "This will be the game of the year,
This will be the game of the year."

Bye bye National Championship
Drove my Chevy to New Orleans but the Tide won the trip
And good ol' boys were drinkin' whiskey and beer
Singin', "This will be the game of the year,
This will be the game of the year."

We started cryin'
We started cryin'

We started cryin'
We started cryin'
(Lyrics © 2000 by Todd A. Sponsler, M.D., from
www.geocities.com/psulionsden. Reprinted by permission.)

A wonderful and dedicated fan base. Access to the best football players in the nation. A strong tradition of winning football. With all of these things in place, is it any wonder Joe Paterno has always loved coaching at Penn State?

Every so often I run into a Trojan fan who wants to tell me that USC were National Champions in 1978. After all, UPI said so. And they had only one loss just like us. And they beat us. But by USC logic, Arizona State, a 9-3 team, would be national champs. Of course, I wouldn't go that far. ASU's coach was Frank Kush, and you already know what I think of him.

Alabama had on our side the AP, momentum, a stronger schedule, and beating Penn State. The Football Writers Association and the National Football Foundation agree. Advantage Alabama: a split vote, but we win the election.

We are the National Champions for 1978.

11

How I Single-Handedly Almost Lost the National Championship

By now you have already learned a great deal about how much time, work, practice, dedication, and effort went into preparing us players for a run at the national championship. What I have touched on is only the beginning. Dedicated coaches and staff members did much more than their contracts called for—more than we or Coach Bryant would have ever demanded—because they realized they were a part of something special. Days, nights, weekends—their lives were Alabama football. The work behind a team like ours is almost unfathomable.

Almost equally unfathomable is the fact that I, a single individual, almost blew it for everyone. I almost lost the national championship all by myself—before we ever had the chance to win it.

It is a sad story of how the greed and avarice of one person can put an entire football team, an entire athletic program for that matter, at risk.

It all started in the spring of 1978, when I got a very mysterious telephone call. The man on the other end of the line identified himself as a "friend" of a famous agent. It seemed that the agent—let's call him "Pinky" for a reason to be revealed later—thought I was the top football player in the nation, and he wanted to talk to me—quietly, of course—in Los Angeles.

In 1978, as today, the NCAA and player agents were not compatible in the world of college football. However, at that time players were not given a great deal of education about how to handle a situation like this should it ever arise. But I did know instinctively that the less I said, the better.

Pinky's "friend" told me that they were sending me two airline tickets to Los Angeles for an upcoming weekend for me and a friend. He went on to say that we would be picked up by a chauffer in a pink Rolls Royce and driven to Pinky's home for our secret discussions. No one in the world would ever know.

A skeptic to the hilt, I said something like, "Sure, OK, I gotta go," and didn't give it another thought. Until, that is, the tickets arrived.

The day they came, I realized that this was a potential problem. A big one. I immediately sent the tickets back to the return address on the envelope. When

Pinky's friend called again, I explained that I felt this would have been against NCAA rules, but I really did appreciate his interest. After that conversation I forgot about the whole situation and concentrated on football. As far as I was concerned it was over for life.

It wasn't.

Summer on campus was a lot of fun. And, even though the NCAA did not allow organized practices, we worked out on our own in large numbers. We all took summer course loads light enough to allow for our workout schedule. We also made sure there was plenty of time to have fun.

In midsummer of 1978, before fall practice began, I got another call from Pinky's friend.

"I am in Tuscaloosa today, with one specific purpose," he said. "I want to talk to you."

Being flattered, I was now in a quandary. This guy had come all the way from LA to see me! I couldn't believe it. He gave me the name of his hotel out by McFarland Mall, on the other side of town (this same hotel was later destroyed by a tornado), and told me to come on out, that he was waiting on me right then.

"What could it hurt?" I rationalized.

I jumped in the car alone and drove to his hotel. When I got there I found what seemed to be a very nice guy in his mid-forties who—even while traveling—had all of the luxuries of life surrounding him. We talked for a while, mostly him telling me how great I was and how I was going to be the first pick in the draft.

At this point I realized he was blowing smoke up my skirt. I tried to excuse myself, telling him that I had several pressing appointments that afternoon, but he stopped me.

"You need to look at this," he said as he pulled a very formal-looking document from his very expensive briefcase.

He handed it over to me and I immediately noticed that *my name* was on the document. It was a contract binding me to him as my agent.

"Sign it today," he said, "and I'll put it in a safe deposit box until after the season ends. No one in the world will ever know."

Although he had not made any specific offer, I knew that there was compensation attached somewhere in that document. And at that moment I realized I could have already gone too far.

Gathering my wits, I told him I was flattered but would wait until the end of my senior year to talk with him further.

"It's now or never, Kid. I'm walking out the door to catch a plane right now."

I shook his hand, purposely not responding, and made a quick exit to my car. As I cranked the car, I realized what I had to do—and I didn't look forward to it. Ten minutes later I pulled into the coliseum parking lot and entered a door that knew was always open. I went straight to Coach Bryant's office. As I approached, heard him on the phone. I forced myself to stand there outside his office when ny instincts said to run. Far and fast.

As he hung up, I knocked on the door frame. He looked up, gave me a little mile, and growled something about coming in and having a seat. "The incredible nrinking couch," I thought, as I headed for the straight-back chair against the wall.

As I began to tell him the story, I realized that his face wasn't showing any emo-ion. I went on and on. Finally I gave him the opportunity to say something.

"Is that all?" he inquired.

"Yes, sir," I responded, now relieved I had unloaded on him.

He immediately picked up the telephone and started dialing. He was calling he NCAA.

When he got the person he wanted on the phone, he introduced the subject and egan to tell the whole story.

"I have a boy in my office," he began, "who just had something happen."

He went on to tell the story—just as I had told him—on and on. Almost word or word.

It was only during this conversation that I realized that the man claiming to e Pinky's "friend" was most likely Pinky himself. I had probably, although un-nowingly, had conversations with an agent, something specifically forbidden by he NCAA.

Coach Bryant's explanation and conversation lasted almost forty-five minutes. oward the end there was a long moment of silence.

"Are we in any trouble?" Coach Bryant asked.

Silence.

"No, he didn't sign anything and he didn't take a trip," Coach responded.

This time I heard a response clearly through Coach Bryant's receiver, which he ad tilted just a little to allow me that opportunity.

"No, sir," was the response. "And reporting this contact immediately is a sub-tantial part of the reason you are not."

Coach Bryant exchanged some pleasantries with the person, then excused him-elf from the conversation saying there was something else he had to do.

He hung up the telephone, jumped up from his desk, and grabbed his beat-up labama baseball cap, heading for the door.

"C'mon," he said, "we'll take care of this guy."

Paul W. Bryant was about to confront an agent who had just jeopardized the future of his football team. It was clearly written in his face now, and he was as mad as I had ever seen him in any locker room. This would not have been pretty.

"He was leaving for the Birmingham Airport as I was leaving," I said. I am sure I sounded relieved.

He put his cap back in its place and sat back down in his chair.

"You did the right thing, Barry. Don't ever worry about coming to me with something like this. Now go find Coach Rutledge and read the NCAA rules on agents."

I did. Had I known this guy was an agent, the University of Alabama and Barry Krauss would have been in big trouble. Had I not told Coach Bryant, and had he not immediately reported the situation, we could have been made to forfeit one or more games. Maybe every game I had ever played in going back to those lawns in Pompano Beach. We could have even been placed on probation for one or more years. I could have been declared ineligible for my senior season.

If I had taken the tickets or signed the contract, there is no end to the hell the NCAA could have rained down on the University of Alabama and me.

The University of Alabama would never have had the chance to win the 1978 national championship. Most probably, the same would have been true for the 1979 championship. My life would have been drastically different.

Coach Bryant had saved me again. He had saved the University of Alabama again, this time from one of its own naive players and an unethical agent.

To my knowledge he never told this story to a soul.

12

Life after the Sugar Bowl

Fast and complicated. Those are the two words that described life after the Sugar Bowl. Much too fast and much more complicated.

It all started right after we got back to school in the spring of 1979. Things moved so fast and became so complicated, so quickly, that there were relationship casualties.

The first was my girlfriend, Amy.

At some point during my senior year Amy and I had become an item. I'm not sure how it happened, but it did.

Don't get me wrong. I am sure I pursued her—probably just like I pursued other girls. I just don't remember the specifics of how Amy and I started our relationship. I must say that my routine was pretty standard: I would flirt with a cute girl in class, at some kind of function, or in a bar. If I could get her number, I might call her a few days later. We would go out once or twice, and she would realize that we were not right for each other. Most girls I dated had goals for a relationship that were just a little different from mine. Some I probably had personality conflicts with, and we mutually dropped our interest for each other. Many had different expectations or perceptions of what I would be like. When I did not meet those perceptions or expectations, nothing followed.

Sure, I just burst that "jocks get all the girls" bubble that seems to have been floating around out there for decades. Boy, was it time for that myth to be put to rest. Normal girls, not the famous and infamous "cleat chasers" Alabama was known for, did not have an inclination to put in the time and effort necessary to date athletes.

Yes, there were a lot of young women who wanted to date football players specifically. There were a lot of girls who accomplished that goal to one degree or another. Perhaps even one of those has since had her own national cable television series. However, those were the girls that we never thought seriously about when we yearned for a real relationship. A real relationship to me was not about jumping in the sack, or going to the right parties, or being seen in certain circles. It was about becoming comfortable with someone in our own time. It was about lying on the floor and watching old movies on television together all Sunday afternoon. It was about cooking dinner together, or going out for lunch between classes, or just coming home to someone who loved you without any qualifications.

All of that stuff was absolutely impossible for us as football players, particularly during football season. From August through December there was almost never a moment that was not already dedicated. When there was some time, it was not the amount or quality on which relationships were built. Of course, I could have made time to go to the Waffle House for dinner or maybe to a movie at some point during the week. Yet even these simple dates had time restrictions written all over them. For example, we almost always had to be in team or position meetings after practice, say until 6:30, or on some days after dinner, and bed check was 11:00. There was no time to do anything.

I had no time—like other students—to laze around on Sunday afternoons with a date. There was no time to go to the Kentuck Arts Festival over in Northport. No time to take a date to a nice dinner, or even to go to Quincy's for a steak and salad.

The real relationship killer for athletes was Bryant Hall. It was always awkward to bring a date whom you really didn't know well to the dorm for lunch on Sunday. I just didn't want to do it. The guys who had long-term relationships prior to coming to college had absolutely no problem with it, but others were like me.

And of course, if you invited a cute new date over to Bryant Hall, it was like throwing food into a catfish pond, causing a great stir from potential other suitors.

Even if you did get into a serious relationship somehow—overcoming all of the odds—there wasn't much time available to build that relationship. Too much was going on, and none of it was conducive to growing personal relationships.

Amy and I did not beat the odds in college. Even though we only met in my senior year, we did make the effort to see each other consistently—dating would be the word outside of football circles—and we did like each other. We made time for each other to the greatest degree possible.

When students returned to the University of Alabama the week after the 1979 Sugar Bowl, everything in the world was different.

The first difference was the demand on my time—as well as Marty's and a few others'. All of a sudden we had agents, and scouts, and all-star game recruiters, and head coaches, and pro team general managers (GMs) calling us. It was bizarre. We were now seemingly different people, totally responsible for our own futures.

Ta Daaaaa! Adults.

Maybe . . . and maybe not.

If we wanted to continue to play football, we had to respond to these requests, all these demands. And of course, that was the only thing we wanted to do.

Amy saw these events as a blatant infringement on our time together. In my mind there was no contest: this was something I had to do.

First up was the East-West Shrine Game, which Marty and I agreed to play. Before we left Alabama, we had come in contact with a virus of some kind and obviously took it with us to the West Coast. We were both sick all week. It really just dropped us. We didn't practice much at all during the entire week. However, we both did manage to play. I wound up being a captain and getting a key interception.

Next was the Senior Bowl. This one was totally business. The first day they made us strip down and walk through what we called a "meat market" for the scouts. They were looking at us for everything: muscle tone, posture, zippers from previous surgeries, even bunions. After that we got down to football. We actually had two practices per day. That way the professional coaching staffs could split their time between the north and south squads.

Believe me, there were a ton of pro scouts and coaches everywhere. Our coaching staff was from the New Orleans Saints, and they worked us hard during the week.

For many guys the Senior Bowl was their first real dramatic exposure to the hundreds of agents who worked the professional football business. Agents were just swarming around all of us. This time it was legal, serious, and totally business.

I did not see Pinky at all. Maybe he already had enough contracts stuffed into that safe deposit box. Or maybe he sent a friend.

After the Senior Bowl it was on to the individual workout phase for different teams. In 1979 there could have possibly been a scouting combine, but I never worked out for one. I did, however, go to workouts for several teams, including Tampa, Miami, Philadelphia, the New York Jets, and Dallas.

Out of this situation came another relationship casualty. I was about to disappoint Coach Bryant for the last time. Because of the demands these workouts placed on our schedule, I dropped out of college. Although Coach Bryant tried to talk me out of making that move—retrospectively, I believe he knew something—I withdrew from the University of Alabama anyway.

Marty Lyons and Tony Nathan did the same.

Most of these professional teams wanted us in there, working out on Friday afternoon, then again on Saturday. Sometimes someone from the team would want to entertain us a day early and encouraged us to fly in on Thursday afternoons.

Those demands, as well as the fact that we knew we were soon to be professional football players, reduced our emphasis on school.

Tony, Marty, and I were lucky enough to travel together on several occasions. Marty and I traveled a lot together.

All of these workouts were pretty similar: I took a physical and did a workout at their direction, which included sprints, pass coverage, lateral movement, and so forth. Then there would be some kind of interview process.

Dallas was different. They were the high-tech team in the NFL. Sure they would time your sprints, put you through some coverage situations, and watch you do some agility drills. But I got the feeling that their primary tests were the ones using technology. For example, they had two computerized hand and foot quickness tests.

The manual quickness and dexterity test required that you strap your hand into a computerized machine with sensor pads the shape of a glove, which had lights above the place for each finger. The pads beneath the fingers were pressure sensitive and the concept was pretty simple: when the light went off, you were to move the corresponding finger. It started slowly, and was easy to follow at first. It went from simple to extremely complex in a short time.

The test for foot speed and lower-body agility was almost the same.

Dallas was the most fun I had at a workout.

Tampa Bay was a close second—but for a different reason.

Tony Nathan, Marty, and I were all invited to Tampa Bay on the same weekend, so we all decided to go together. Of course, as usual, the club picked up our flight expenses.

When we got to the Tampa airport, there was no one to pick us up, so we rented a car and went out to dinner . . . a really nice dinner. Obviously, our thinking was that the Tampa Bay Buccaneers were getting a really great deal to look at us three Alabama boys together. Our meal cost close to $400 for the three of us—in 1979.

The next day we went for our workout and put in a really hard day. We also turned in our expenses. By the time we got back to the hotel the team general manager had called ahead of us and had the hotel manager lock up Tony Nathan's stuff. (He was trying to confiscate everyone's luggage, but Marty and I had packed up that morning and dumped our stuff into the car.)

It seemed that the GM was mad at us because of our meal expense. He told us curtly that we were on a per diem meal allowance, and that we would have to pay the Buccaneers back before Mr. Nathan's bags were released.

Thank goodness Tony had a credit card and could use it to bail us out. We laughed about that situation for years.

All three of us just loved beating the Bucs after that day.

In our travels together Marty and I had a lot of time to talk about any number of things, from the NFL teams who needed us the most to the agents we thought were the least harmful and most helpful. We decided to use the same agent, Marvin Blank, from Atlanta.

To this day I cannot tell you why we made that decision. He seemed like a nice enough guy, but he did not have any headliners' names that we wanted to follow.

Quite honestly, I was courted heavily by Joe Namath's agent, who was widely considered the best agent in football. He even flew me to Youngstown, Ohio, to meet him and a couple of his clients, including Rocky Blier. I was more in awe of Rocky than the agent, although I knew he had to be good.

The three-and-a-half months from January 1 to the draft just flew by.

I went home to Pompano a few days prior to the NFL draft, accompanied by my agent, Marvin Blank. On Saturday morning, just around 8:00 a.m., I received a call from Ted Marchibroda. He asked if I still wanted to be a Baltimore Colt, to which I responded affirmatively with some kind of expletive for emphasis, I'm sure.

"Great Barry, Bob Irsay wants to talk to you."

"We're drafting you with our first pick in the first round. Congratulations!" Irsay said.

I couldn't believe it. I had just been chosen in the first round of the NFL draft.

Irsay sent his private jet to Pompano for me within the hour—they wanted me in Baltimore to meet the press. Marvin and I packed up and within two hours I was on the way to Baltimore and life as a professional football player.

The previous year Tony Dorsett had been a first rounder and got $1 million in a six-year deal. Back then, the teams tried to obfuscate their deals with players. Details of specific deals only came out rarely, but Dorsett's was on the public record. Marvin said he wanted to get the same terms for me as Tony got, plus a substantial signing bonus. Once discussions started, they didn't last too long. Baltimore and Irsay wanted to sign me quickly. We got the $1 million over six years, plus a $300,000 signing bonus.

I was living a dream.

13

Welcome to the NFL

On the morning of January 1, 1979, any number of teams in the NFL needed line-backers. My 4.6-second speed in the forty-yard dash, in a 6'3", 242-pound body only placed me in the top half of the prospects. I was projected to go in the seventh round of the draft.

However, God didn't take that New Year's Day off. He was hard at work for young Richard Barry Krauss.

Like millions of other Americans, Bob Irsay, owner of the Baltimore Colts, was watching the Sugar Bowl game. The Colts, Irsay later said, needed a strong middle linebacker to anchor their defense of the future. As the story goes, I was not on Irsay's radar screen until The Goal Line Stand.

As previously discussed, Baltimore used its first-round draft pick to choose me. I was the second linebacker taken in the first round, the overall sixth pick in the 1979 NFL draft.

Other coaches, owners, and players were also watching—a fact that would pay off for me years down the road.

Although I did not know it, there was one coach in particular whose belief and confidence in me would be a guiding light, though sometimes from afar, through-out my career. That coach was George Hill.

George Hill was the longtime defensive coordinator under Coach Woody Hayes at Ohio State. On January 2, 1978, after the 1977 season, Alabama had played Ohio State in the Sugar Bowl, and I had met George the week before the game. We also talked again just briefly after the game, when we had beaten Ohio State 35-6.

At the end of the 1978 season a frustrated Ohio State team accepted a bid to play in the Gator Bowl on December 31, the night before our Sugar Bowl game with Penn State. George Hill's career, like mine, was about to take a fateful turn. But unlike my bowl appearance, the circumstances George faced that weekend were less than positive.

The football coach succession plans at Ohio State were already in place, ap-proved by the decision makers at every level. When Woody Hayes retired, George

Hill would take over as Ohio State head coach, assuming one of the most prestigious positions in college football.

Late in the Gator Bowl against Clemson, Charlie Bauman, a Clemson defensive player, intercepted an Ohio State pass and headed for the sidelines. An irate Woody Hayes, caught up in the fury and frustration of losing the game, saw Bauman coming and swung hard at him, catching him across the collarbone.

The national television cameras caught it all. Woody and his staff would soon catch the brunt of the responsibility.

Before the Ohio State airplane touched down in Columbus, Woody Hayes had been fired. Ohio State administrators sought and found a new head coach with Ohio State ties but outside of the Hayes system. Earl Bruce, a former Buckeye player and assistant coach, took over the reins. George Hill—totally innocent—had his future swept away by circumstances beyond his control. But his misfortune would eventually benefit me.

What I didn't know when I was drafted was that my trip through the NFL would start out a little rockier than I had envisioned.

When I got to camp, I began to feel that the well had been poisoned for me. No one welcomed me initially. I was not accepted by the team at all, no matter how hard I worked. This was a totally new experience for me—and something I had not expected.

The Baltimore Colts had a veteran defensive club with some very big names. One of those big names was Ed Simonini, a middle linebacker from Texas A&M University. He was the guy I was to replace. There were a couple of problems with that thought process: Ed Simonini wasn't ready to go; his defensive teammates weren't ready for him to go; and, most interesting, his coaches weren't ready for him to go.

It seems that I had been Bob Irsay's pick. The owner wanted me. Nobody else did. Trouble lay ahead.

The Colts were two years removed from their defensive heyday when I was drafted, but they didn't yet know, or wouldn't acknowledge, that fact. In the seasons from 1975 to 1977 the defensive line, composed of Fred Cook, Joe Ehrman, and Mike Barnes, was known as the Sack Pack. After 1977 they pretty much fell apart. Nothing was the same. Yet the veterans were hanging on.

Of course, I walked into this situation completely blind. The one thing I did know was that I wasn't getting the fair shot I thought I deserved.

The Colts and the Philadelphia Eagles had a training camp tradition of holding several scrimmages each year at Goucher College in Baltimore. That year, Philadelphia's head coach, Dick Vermeil, had hired a new defensive coordinator—George Hill.

Trying to prove myself worthy of the first-round choice, and battling the nonbelievers inside my own defense, I played extremely hard all the time. George Hill even made a point of telling me he was impressed, not only at my play but also by how I was handling the sticky political situation at Baltimore.

As camp moved ahead, several of the veterans made it their business to prove I had been a "wasted draft choice." In this quest they did not give up: they worked on it all season.

In my rookie year at Baltimore we lost eleven games, five more games than Alabama had lost in all four years that I played there. That was something else I had not expected.

My life as a rookie on the field was a living hell. As this soap opera was unfolding around me, I found myself isolated, completely on my own, and even ostracized. My roommate, Steve Heimkreiter—a linebacker from Notre Dame—was still living the college life, so he was no help. I was lonely and deeply in need of someone who would support me and care for me even in the worst of times, which these obviously were.

At this point Amy reentered the picture. After the whirlwind of the draft had swept me up into this new life, Amy and I had only sporadic contact. As camp began, she and I began to talk more consistently. Soon, I was flying her into Baltimore for home games and long weekends. She was someone who could give me the comfort, the confidence, and the enthusiasm I needed to go out every day and try to take on the whole world. This continued throughout my rookie year, until we—once again—agreed to disagree. She had one set of priorities and I another. We broke up toward the end of the season.

To top it off, I rolled an ankle in the Philadelphia game and was injured for basically the rest of the year.

Still, my problems were minor compared to the team's problems. In the midst of this nightmare of a season, the team morale, camaraderie, and spirit drained slowly from the 1979 Baltimore Colts. There were vicious fights, racial divides, and individual feuds that made the game of football seem like work. Someone—the coaches, the owner, or the GM—needed to clean house. But no one wanted to run off the veterans who had been key to winning Baltimore's three consecutive Eastern Division titles from 1975 to 1977.

Our problem, I believe, started at the top—our owner, Bob Irsay. Don't get me wrong, Bob Irsay was a good owner. He was a dynamic and charismatic man who was never afraid to make a decision. However, some players, including me, believed he made too many decisions—and sometimes from an emotional viewpoint. Bob Irsay did not have the rapport with his coaches that he should have had. The coaches were afraid to give him key pieces of information about the team and its players. They believed that if they did this, they would be giving up some of their autonomy. Bob saw them not making decisions and knew something was wrong. So he jumped in. And, without the proper information, he made decisions that were ill-founded or illogical.

For example, in an important and hard-fought game late in the year, our kicker, Tony Lenhardt, missed a field goal that would have given us the win. Everyone was distraught and depressed, but no one was holding anything against Lenhardt—that stuff just happens occasionally. Hell, he was a good kicker. Just like a star receiver dropped a ball occasionally, kickers missed kicks sometimes. After the game Bob Irsay entered the locker room and announced, "If Tony Lenhardt isn't a Colt, no one is!" trying to show his support for our teammate. Somewhere between that night and the following day, some person—coach, GM, or player—got to Bob. They convinced him, gave him some piece of information that changed his mind.

The next day Tony was fired.

Although the picture I paint is bleak, let me say here—to borrow a phrase from another Alabama boy, Jimmy Buffett—"things were better off than I had feared." Retrospectively, with all things considered, I had a very good rookie year *on the field*. I had broken into the starting lineup, despite the fact that no one originally wanted me there. I had also led the team in tackles and had come back completely from my ankle injury.

Even more important, I had learned more of the professional game—some of the techniques of pass coverage, the intricacies of reading offenses, and the power of being a leader.

I had also met and played against some of the greatest football players who ever lived, and I was honored to be on the same field with them. In fact, on my first trip to Pittsburgh I got to meet some of my all-time heroes. I was totally enthralled. Warming up I saw Terry Bradshaw, Lynn Swann, John Stallworth, Rocky Blier, Franco Harris, Mike Webster, and Jack Lambert. That day I ran toward Lynn Swann just to introduce myself, and I tripped on the turf and slid up to his feet. As I was getting up to shake his hand, he said something like, "Dumb rookie."

I didn't care. It was wonderful. Even today I love to talk about those times And I do!

People ask me about everything. Which NFL team was the toughest? Who was the best running back? What was the best quarterback-receiver combination?

That last one is easy.

My weekends in the NFL were always challenging. But my weeks were worse During practice I had the pleasure of trying to cover Joe Washington as Bert Jones a pretty fair QB from LSU, was throwing darts to him. I have to say, though, that Joe Washington was the reason I became a good pass defender. He juked, and jagged, and zigzagged his way to the top of the NFL, so he was a great teacher for me. Covering Joe Washington in practice probably extended my career by years My own teammates were the best quarterback-receiver combination in the NFL.

I am not so sure about who I think was the best running back I played against They were all great. Each had something that the others didn't. Some juked and jived, some just steamrolled you, others did everything.

For me the best backs were the ones who I could never get a solid lick on. Marcus Allen, Tony Dorsett, Barry Sanders, and even Earl Campbell were at the top of that category. Even directly in the hole they might turn just a bit or be spinning at impact as I hit them, and I never felt that I got them squarely.

Yes, things really were "better off than I had feared."

As a rookie, I had made some great friends and allies. I also had some good times that year.

One of those great friends and allies was Bert Jones, the LSU quarterback from the early 1970s. He was a super nice guy, and his acceptance of me and my play was one of the things that tipped the balance of my personal accomplishments that season toward the positive side of the scale. He went out of his way to set an example for the other vets.

In fact, one of the most memorable moments of my rookie year was due to Bert and several other veterans taking me with them on a "hunting trip," a privilege totally unheard of for rookies. I had never experienced anything like this in the woods of Alabama. We loaded into a van, with a Colts equipment man driving The first stop was the liquor store. "Loaded guns and alcohol," I thought. That was a combination always sure to generate some excitement. The veterans bought several cases of beer, some of which we consumed on the way to the country. By the time we drove up to the huge three-story barn in the middle of nowhere, our condition had deteriorated substantially. However, the guys at the barn were "pros" in the hunting business. They clearly had done this before. They positioned each of us at different places around the barn, with our backs to the walls. The next thing I knew, the windows upstairs flew open and pheasants were flying out. POW, POW. BAM, BAM! The vets were having a blast. The pheasants—once thrown from the windows—had to fly for their lives. It sounded like a war zone. Here we were, all lined up around this barn just blasting these birds—and they called this hunting.

We drank beer and blasted birds for probably two hours, until we ran out of shells.

Although it sounds horrible, for busy and extremely stressed guys who loved to hunt prior to their life in the pros, this was heaven. Too much fun was had that day for these pages. Let's just say it ended only after a veteran's tooth was lost and had to be surgically reimplanted into its owner's mouth.

Bert Jones appeared later that year on *The American Sportsman* TV show. You can imagine how much hell we "pheasant hunters" gave him when that show aired. American sportsman, my ass! I constantly threatened to expose him for the real hunter I knew him to be.

At the end of my rookie year I made a trip back to Tuscaloosa for some type of formal banquet and was seated by Coach Bryant. It was the first time we had spoken in an adult-to-adult relationship, and he was a true delight to be around. He was personable, and kind, and thoughtful . . . I realized he really valued my friendship.

He was slapping me on the back, laughing, and cutting up like I had never seen before. This surely was a different man than the one I knew from the tower. But I enjoyed him. I liked him. And he liked me. Yeah, I loved him. He was embracing me as a person, not as his pupil or his player.

While the banquet was still going on, I whispered the Bert Jones story to him, and we just howled like a couple of eighteen-year-olds.

As soon as the festivities were over, he pulled me aside.

"I ain't told hardly nobody this huntin' story, 'cause hardly anyone's gonna believe it. But I once killed two turkeys with one shot," he said proudly. "You can pass that on to your Cajun hunter friend Mr. Jones."

Bear Bryant had won yet another competition, one-upped a fellow hunter. And an LSU guy, no less.

From that day on Coach Bryant and I were friends. Although I did not get back to Tuscaloosa as often as I wanted to, I did manage to go by and see him every time

I was in town. And he wanted to see me; he almost demanded that I stop by his office when I was in town.

THE MIKE MCCORMACK ERA

The following year offered even greater challenges. In January 1980 Coach Marchibroda was fired and replaced by Mike McCormack.

In Mike's first year we posted a 7-9 record, a slight improvement from the previous year. However, the dissension and trouble inside the team seemed to escalate during Mike's tenure. Much of that trouble was due to the incredible pressures an NFL coach experiences. A lot of it was due to Mike's own personal style.

The media and the public also put a great deal of pressure on the shoulders of a team's first-round draft choices. Hell, everyone wanted winning franchises. Unfortunately, since on average only half of the teams in the league can win, it was understandable that the other half would be very uncomfortable, perhaps even irate.

First-round draft choices, coaches, offensive and defensive coordinators, and general managers often got to be the scapegoats.

If that was not bad enough, when the Baltimore Colts didn't win, Mike McCormack was quick to pass the buck and make scapegoats of his players. The one time he tried to hang a loss directly on me, he had his facts so wrong—and the right people knew it—he wound up hurting only himself.

This story begins on a Wednesday night, after practice, when Alex Hawkins, a former Colt, Johnny Unitas, and Bobby Boyd came by practice and invited me to Johnny's and Bobby's restaurant, The Golden Arm, for dinner. I was running late getting off the training table, and by the time I got there, the guys had already eaten, Unitas was heading out the door, and Bobby and Alex were in the back shooting craps or rolling nickels. After dinner I joined them at the bar and soaked up many of their stories from the glory days of professional football. I got in about 3:00 a.m. on Thursday.

Not a problem. As nights on the town for the pros go, this one was sedate—sitting around with two older guys listening to their football stories, laughing like hell.

Sunday came around and we had another bad game. I made a mental error that cost us a field goal, but the game was already out of control.

In the locker room after the game, Mike McCormack called me out.

"This loss can be blamed on Barry Krauss for laying out all night last night."

I could not believe my ears. Somehow, McCormack had heard the story of Wednesday and believed it happened on Saturday. Choosing discretion, I let it slide until I knew for sure exactly what he was talking about.

Subsequently, I made damn sure that everyone who mattered—including Bob Irsay—knew the truth, as verified by Johnny Unitas, Alex Hawkins, and Bobby Boyd. In Baltimore you didn't get better allies than these guys.

That was the last time Coach McCormack called my number in that situation. We finished the 1981 season with a franchise-worst record of 2-14.

The Dawning of the Frank Kush Era

On December 21, 1981, the Colts named Frank Kush to replace McCormack as head coach. Irsay named Ernie Accorsi as the new general manager. Ernie was a rising star in the NFL and no doubt helped Frank stay in place as long as he did.

You already know a great deal about my relationship with Frank Kush. What I haven't told you yet was that Frank Kush was a smart man. He surrounded himself with other smart men. Eventually, one of those smart men was a defensive coordinator named George Hill.

This was the first chance I had to get to know George well. After only a short time we both realized that I could run his defensive scheme almost perfectly. I called all the plays and was the on-field coordinator. We thought alike. We worked alike. We believed in each other. Our relationship was excellent from day one. I wish I could say the same for our record.

The 1982 season was a strike-shortened year in which we played only nine games. We went 0-8-1.

It was a tragedy of tremendous proportions, but it opened the door to getting us the first pick in the 1983 draft. But before the draft, there was another tragedy I had to endure.

Losing a Legend

On January 26, 1983, I got a call from Marty Lyons in New York. Coach Bryant had died. Marty was still the first to know. I dropped everything and made arrangements to get back to Tuscaloosa for the funeral.

Much had transpired between Coach Bryant and me since I had left school campus in 1979.

After I returned to Tuscaloosa in my rookie year and was met with such a warm reception from Coach Bryant, I tried to get back as much as possible. Most of the time it was not during football season, so both Coach and I had less pressure on us. Sometimes, during football season, I would call him. He always made time to talk to me.

I did notice that he seemed to become substantially more frail every time I talked with him or saw him.

In the 1980s it seemed that every time I would go down to Tuscaloosa, Dr. DeShazo had admitted him to the hospital. It happened on many occasions; I would go to Druid City Hospital, as it was known then, and sit in the room with Mrs. Bryant and the coach. We would talk about almost anything . . . sometimes everything. Billy Varner, Coach Bryant's driver, was there on many occasions. In the later years those two were inseparable.

Although none of these visits ever had a specific purpose, they all had a huge impact on me: they made me feel like a member of his family. I will treasure those moments forever.

At the funeral a large number of former players were his honorary pallbearers. His current players were his official pallbearers. The funeral was the most phenomenal tribute to a man I have ever seen. It was held in four or five churches—the service was electronically linked from the primary church to the others, all overflowing.

As we loaded our cars for the funeral procession, it struck me that there was a huge number of people on the streets that cold, wet winter day. Sure enough, as the procession rolled onto campus and down the street past Bryant-Denny and the Coliseum, the onlookers were sometimes three or four deep.

The interstate, I-59/20, for the sixty miles from Tuscaloosa to Birmingham, was basically shut down—our northbound procession was miles long, and throngs of drivers in the southbound lanes pulled over to the roadside and stopped to pay their respects. There must have been twenty-five state trooper cars in and around the motorcade. People—fans—were on the overpasses with homemade signs that spoke of their prayers, admiration, and well-wishes for Coach and his family. One sign was particularly poignant: "God Needed an Offensive Coordinator."

Once we were at Elmwood Cemetery in Birmingham, it became apparent just how many former players had dropped everything and come to pay their respects to their coach.

That Coach Bryant died so soon after his final football game was not surprising to us. He lived for football. He lived for Alabama.

The 1983 Draft

As the Colts first pick of 1979, I always looked forward to each subsequent draft. Every year meant that the pressure of being a first-round draft pick was getting farther and farther behind me. The Baltimore Colts' NFL draft debacle of 1983 removed all pressure from all previous number-one picks. If the history of the NFL was written today, this Colts draft would be at the top as the worst draft decisions ever made.

On April 26, 1983, the Colts chose John Elway as the first pick in the draft. The Colts did this after repeatedly being warned by John and his agent that he would never play a down in a Baltimore Colts uniform. Under the threat of being banned from the NFL, Elway threatened to play minor league baseball, or even jump to the USFL, and give up his right to play in the NFL. The Colts drafted him anyway.

Elway steadfastly refused to even consider an offer from the Colts.

Finally, the bell went off in everyone's head—the John Elway thing wasn't going to happen, and the longer the team dilly-dallied, the less value the Elway pick had. So the Colts traded Elway to Denver in return for their first-round choice, offensive lineman Chris Hinton, a quarterback from Purdue named Mark Herrmann, and a later first-round choice. To this day, people affiliated with the Colts organization will talk about how Chris Hinton went on to make the Pro Bowl that year, trying to make this elephant of a mistake more palatable.

Finally the pressure was off. I had hoped it would have been removed in some other fashion—like winning the Super Bowl—but I was still relieved. The Colts front office had so botched this situation that there was no possible way any of us previous first-rounders could be blamed for anything other than working for idiots.

It was a huge relief . . . so big that it made me bearable from a personal perspective. That was important to Amy, who had moved to Baltimore to be with me in 1981. We were married in 1982. Our off-again, on-again relationship was on again. It was a good thing. In 1983 my first daughter, Ashley, was born. Boy did that event bring about some change.

Our 1983 season was a welcome change, too. We posted what was, at the time, the biggest turnaround for a winless team in NFL history. We went 7-9 for the season, after a fine start of 6-4.

The relief of our success was team-wide. We even rubbed it in a little on some of our most severe critics. One reporter for the *Baltimore Sun,* Vito Stellino, who

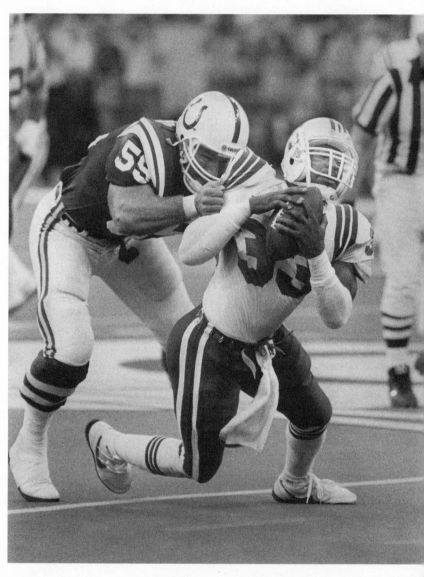

Barry wrangles and wrestles the Patriots' Tony Collins to the ground. (Photo by Donald Larson)

was always on the field milling around the players, found himself constantly being "accidentally" hit with footballs. He caught on quickly and realized he was "too close to the story."

As soon as the season ended, Bob Irsay began to shop for a new home for the Colts. He had discussions with several cities. The two main suitors were Indianapolis and Phoenix, and he had basically turned it into a bidding war. Now understanding that Bob Irsay was serious, the Maryland state legislature began to craft legislation that would use eminent domain laws to make the Colts remain in Baltimore. Irsay's chief asset was about to be frozen in Baltimore. On March 28, 1984, Phoenix pulled out, and Bob called Indianapolis officials to tell them he was on the way—but they couldn't announce it just yet.

At just after midnight that same day Bob and Jim Irsay (father and son, now president and general manager, respectively) moved the Baltimore Colts to Indianapolis.

14

New Life in Indianapolis

The absolute best thing about the first year in Indianapolis is that it was Frank Kush's last year as our coach. His combined record with the Colts was a horrific 11-28-1.

He was fired prior to the end of the year, and our interim coach, Hal Hunter, led us to two wins at the season's end.

One of my greatest accomplishments that year was my small part in helping Frank Kush leave. The other was getting to know and work with George Hill.

Indianapolis was (and is) a wonderful place. I fell in love with the Hoosier Dome (later to be named the RCA Dome) and loved to play there.

The people of Indiana embraced our team, and the players as individuals, immediately.

Although our records the first years didn't show a big improvement from the Baltimore years, we had a much better football team in Indianapolis. Rod Dowhower took over as head coach in 1985, and we went 5-11 that year. Rod was a great guy, but the stress of coaching in the NFL weighed heavily on him. He even passed out on the sideline during one of our games.

In the middle of the 1986 season Ron Meyer took over the helm from Rod.

But enough about wins and losses. They are only a mark of the success of teams and their coaches.

Playing football—playing professional football—was wonderful.

Did I want to win? Absolutely, I did!

But I still enjoyed football no matter how many games my teams won or lost. I loved everything about the game: the venues (particularly the Hoosier Dome), the people who worked at the stadiums around the country, the big hits, the fans, the broadcasters, and the fans. Did I mention the fans?

I also loved playing against my old friends from Alabama and my old rivals from the SEC.

These guys were some of the best in the business.

That brings me back to Marty Lyons. As discussed earlier, Marty and I were always in some type of competition. We could be walking back from class and we would break into a sprint, trying simply to beat each other.

Once, on a road trip to New York to play the Jets, I extended that competition into our professional careers. As you have no doubt noticed, when an NFL game is out of reach, there is not a lot of real drama on extra point attempts. In some cases guys virtually lean against each other and have a short chat. This was the first time I had been afforded the opportunity to actually line up against Marty in the pros, since we were both defensive players.

As we approached the line of scrimmage, Marty greeted me as I expected, "Hi ya, man, how have you been?"

"Not bad," I responded nonchalantly, as I dragged—almost moped—into my three-point stance.

I could tell from his stance—he had no weight on his hand—that he was unprepared for me to actually hit him. Then he looked away and started business as usual. At the snap I just creamed him. As I was running off the field I looked over my shoulder to see that he was getting up and running after me. He was pissed.

I went deep into our bench area and pretended to be busy. All the while Marty was looking for me, yelling my name combined with other bad words.

"What did you do to that guy?" was the question from my teammates.

Of course, the Colts were having another really bad day. The Jets scored again. This time Marty was ready.

"Bring it on, pal!" was probably close to his verbal challenge.

"I'm coming, big guy," could have been my response.

Well, I lined up in a three-point stance, leaning heavily on my hand like I was going to fire out strong to take him on.

He did the same. This would be some unusual type of a clash on an extra point.

Just prior to their snapping the ball, I relaxed. At the snap I jumped out of the way and Marty sprang toward where I was . . . or had been . . . and ate a bunch of field sliding toward the end zone.

I hurried to the sideline again. He came after me again, madder than ever. He stayed mad about that one for a couple of years. Only after I explained that it was for all of his jokes on me over all those years did he forgive me. But sometimes I catch myself looking over my shoulder when I hear a noise behind me . . .

Think about this nightmare. You're in the NFL, and you have to play a team with a coach very much like Coach Bryant. It executes the fundamentals perfectly and will just line up and shove the ball down your throat. Then add a cat-quick Tony Nathan to the recipe, cutting so hard that his butt is less than six inches off the ground, who also runs exquisite pass routes. Last, give them the best quarterback in the history of the NFL, Dan Marino, and you have the Miami Dolphins of my era. What a headache.

Southeastern Conference rivalries had a way of extending into the NFL. I simply hated playing the Buffalo Bills for two reasons: they always seemed to have our number, and they had Joe Cribbs.

It wasn't enough that we had to live with and beat an Auburn team every year with phenomenal talent like Joe Cribbs. I got to see the guy at least twice a year for years. He was even quicker, smarter, and a better blocker than he was in college.

Terry Robiskie, Charles Alexander, James Brooks, Stanley Morgan, and William Andrews—I got to see them all . . . over and over again. You think they were great in college? Just throw in a whole bunch of bigger, quicker, faster blockers, and you can begin to envision how hard the job of a linebacker might be on any Sunday afternoon.

Stanley Morgan, formerly of the University of Tennessee, and the Patriots had our number, just like Buffalo and Cribbs. Looking back on my career, one Stanley Morgan play was particularly painful for me. In the pros everybody was accounted for, at all times, on the field. That goes double on punt returns. Not only did they have your number, but they knew where you were, where you were going, and how quickly you could get there. If you were lucky and fast, you might be able to outrun a blocking assignment. If the receiver was cagey, he could overcome your speed with a little misdirection. Once, at New England, I had a perfect bead on Stanley Morgan. He took the punt, drifted to one side, then reversed field on me. I turned only a little before I knew he had thrown me right into his wall of blockers. As I was still turning, I got ear-holed—that's getting hit so hard from the side that it feels like the blocker has come straight through your helmet and slammed directly into your brain. It was an experience only comparable to stepping out of your nice, warm shower in the morning and being hit by an asteroid. I was hurt so badly that I did well just to get off the field.

But no matter how much pain was involved, I still loved the game!

Throughout my career—in Baltimore, Indy, and Miami—I was almost always the first player to get to the stadium and the last player to leave. In Indianapolis, if we had a noon or 1:00 p.m. game, I would be at the Dome by 9:00 a.m. I would go out on the turf and walk around, loosening up. I would throw the football up in the stands to the sweepers and cleaners. Usually they would throw it back! No, they were all great. We would play catch, back and forth, with me on the field going around the stadium. I would walk up into the stands and around the Dome. I would go up in the press box to see what was going on up there.

After those home games I would always find a reason to stay. I would ice my knees or my shoulders and lie on the training table to catch the late games or the scores from around the league. Finally I would take a long shower, then take my time getting dressed.

My pattern has a simple explanation: I was breathing in the life of football. I knew that this wonderful, rare, and sweet breath was limited. I wanted to take it all in and enjoy it, and live it, while I could.

Finally, as the RCA Dome staff was trying to lock the doors, I would exit the building and partake in still another custom that was pro football. I headed to a faraway gravel parking lot, which always held a single green van and the last Colts fans on the property. I called it the Green Van Fan Club. I made a point of stopping by their encampment after every game as if to say, "Carry on, fans, carry on." They came to expect me, and I tried never to disappoint them. We would have a beer together and maybe a bowl of chili or whatever their concoction of that day might have been. They were always there, always happy to see me.

Road games were different. Road games were for road warriors. Team schedules were sacrosanct, inflexible. Catch the plane, catch the bus, catch the hotel food and then a bed, catch the bus, play the game, catch the bus, catch the plane.

In my early years the team did some little things to try to make the schedules bearable. For example, as soon as you got on the bus after the game, they would give you a small bag that contained a little ice and two or three beers. After the high-stress, high-impact day at the office, there was nothing better. We would get on the airplane, drink those beers and relax on the way home.

That practice came to a screeching halt after one NFL head coach, a tight end in his playing days, was arrested on the drive home from the airport. It seems that he had gotten his hands on several of those little bags of beer and was clearly DUI.

Leave it to the NFL to make work seem more like work.

Not too many road trips later, I got together with our two equipment managers, Jon Scott and Chris Matlock, and formulated a plan to bring sanity back to road games. On road games every team rented an equipment truck in which all of the equipment was loaded for the trips from the airport to the stadium prior to the game and back to the airport after the game. Prior to reloading the truck after the

Barry clowns with a "dog bone" thrown at him by the fans in the "dog pound" in Cleveland. (Photo by Donald Larson)

game, Jon and Chris would order pizza or sausage for a snack, and a few beers. They would throw them in the back of the truck after the equipment was loaded. I would slip off the bus and ride in the back of the truck with them, chowing down, as we were heading to the airport.

Soon this practice turned into a tradition. Our equipment guys would host visiting equipment guys and vice versa. One or two select players got to ride along and partake of the goodies.

Several years later I introduced the tradition to the Miami Dolphins at a time when Dan Marino was in the white-hot national media spotlight for never winning a Super Bowl. Marino was an instant member of the fraternity of the "Boys of Iced Beer." He brought in Jim Jensen and Mike Reckenbach.

Our equipment manager at Miami, Bob Monica, became famous for the delicious food and gracious accoutrements he provided to other teams, including homemade Italian sausage, Cuban cigars, and special beer. Thereafter, we would benefit from those teams' reciprocity.

Marino, dressed as usual in the finest of suits, would climb over dirty, stinking uniform and equipment bags, and plop down in the midst of it all. Once settled in, he would open a beer. Jensen went for the food first. Reckenbach and I would light big cigars, then go for the food and the beer.

The national media, which the Dolphins always allowed on their team bus, were asking, "Where's Marino? Where is Dan?"

In most cases we were only a couple of car lengths away, but we were enjoying delicious food and drink, having fun. Marino never missed the media coverage. Coach Shula acted like he didn't know what was happening.

Everyone was happy except the media. They always thought they had gotten on the wrong bus because when they got on the airplane, Marino was already there.

Back to Indianapolis. And reality.

In 1986, out of the clear blue sky, Amy approached me one afternoon and announced that she wanted a divorce.

Sometimes life's bombs can set our lives on a new, better, and more productive course.

Being Barry Krauss, I did not see any possible good in this situation at first.

Reluctantly, I began to look for a divorce lawyer. Unfortunately, a lot of the Colts had used them, so references were abundant. I had heard good things about a firm called Buck, Berry, Landau, Breunig and Quinn, so I decided to talk to them.

At our first meeting we discussed generally what the situation was with Amy and Ashley, and we agreed to meet again later in the week. On the way out my lawyer asked if he could introduce me to one of the firm's partners—a huge Colts fan. Of course I agreed and was introduced to Jim Quinn.

Jim was an unusual guy. After talking about ten minutes or so—and having just a grand time—he reached into his desk and pulled out a piece of paper.

"It's my obituary," he said smiling, as he handed it across the desk.

Several years earlier Jim had been involved in a horrible motorcycle accident and sustained very grave injuries. In a deep coma, and with drastic head and neck injuries, everyone thought he would most certainly die. Therefore his obituary was written in preparation for its run in the *Indianapolis Star*. But he came out of the coma and began to recover.

When he was shown that obituary, the story of his life, it became the turning point he needed to evaluate and change his life. The man I met was truly a live-for-the-moment guy, who realized how precious life is and was living it to the fullest.

As we talked, I noticed the picture of a beautiful young lady on the credenza behind him. I couldn't help but stare at her as we went on and on.

He obviously noticed.

"That's my daughter, Darcy."

"She's gorgeous," I blathered.

"Thank you," he replied. "I think she is too. Would you like to meet her? She's single."

I realized my eyes were widening in anticipation just before I stammered, "Sure!"

"I'll give her a call and introduce you two."

Over the next several weeks we were supposed to meet six or seven times . . . something simple at first, just to try to get to know each other. It never came off. She was going in hundreds of directions, and I was busy too . . . There were always excuses. Finally, after weeks of broken and rescheduled dates, Darcy Quinn and I sat down for dinner. Three hours later, when we got up from that table, I had found my soul mate.

Ahhh, but hold on a minute. Barry Krauss—being Barry Krauss—could not have something this good happen to him without something equally bad happening. Or worse!

In the fourth week of the 1986 season the New York Jets (there's Marty again) came to the RCA Dome to play our Indianapolis Colts.

At some point in the game I twisted my knee on the turf. I was never really sure how I had done it. To me it seemed that it was not a very bad injury. But the orthopedist saw torn cartilage, and I immediately had arthroscopic surgery.

While the doc was in there, he discovered that my anterior cruciate ligament (ACL) was also torn—a career-ending injury in many cases. The next Monday, after returning from San Francisco with the team, I had major reconstructive surgery.

All of this stuff was bad enough, but I was also going through the divorce. When I thought things couldn't get any worse, the Big Guy Upstairs proved me wrong.

While I was in the hospital, I got a very serious infection. I had to go back under the knife for that immediately. At this point I had undergone three operations in four weeks.

The news was still bad. After the surgery the doctors told me it did not go as well as they had hoped.

"We might have to amputate the leg," they said, much too coldly and clinically.

They agreed to give medication one last chance prior to going on to the next step. They surgically inserted an antibiotic shunt—a catheter in my vein—so I could constantly be given the antibiotic medicine every six hours. How my body responded to the antibiotics would determine my future.

I found myself lying in a hospital bed with my life a wreck, my career seemingly over, and doctors talking about amputating my leg. This was the lowest of the low for me.

My response was to crawl out of bed and—very carefully—get on my knees and pray; pray for my life, my career. Pray simply for God to pick me up.

If I had known it was that simple, I would have done it long before then. Boy, did He *ever* pick me up. He was working on the project already.

Darcy and I had been seeing each other for several weeks. While I was in the hospital, she was there every day.

Lying in bed I realized that this beautiful and loving young woman could not be attracted to what she saw in front of her. God, the Big Guy Upstairs, was responsible.

It took some time, but I recovered. Darcy was with me all the way. She inspired me and encouraged me not to give up. Once I got out of the hospital, I knew everything was going to be all right. I committed myself to proving the skeptics wrong—there were a lot of folks, coaches and players both, who said I would never be back.

Then there was Tom Zupancic, the Colts strength coach, who made my comeback his own personal goal. A mountain of a man—another in my life who also wrestled a bear and won—he was a weight-lifting fiend. He could move mountains, and he did in my case.

I rehabbed hard—working out twice a day—and I took care of my knees like never before. Soon the pain was limited and the motion unlimited. I kept working. I had plenty of time from the fourth game of one season to camp of the next season: nine months. By the time I reported to camp for the 1987 season, I was in the best physical shape I had ever been. I was bigger and faster than ever—268 pounds and could sometimes break 4.6 in the forty.

God had remade my life—given me another chance. The journey from here on would be with Darcy.

In the 1987 season I became known as one of the best coverage linebackers in the league. Our defense was tough, and our offense was growing better by the week. That year I won the Ed Block Courage Award for my comeback from the devastating knee injuries and surgical complications.

That year we were 9-6 and won the Eastern Division.

The following year held great promise for the Indianapolis Colts.

I worked out hard in my preparation in the off-season. As the 1988 season began, I felt I was better than ever. I was looking forward to a great year—the last on my current contract with the Colts.

However, as the season progressed, something was going on in Ron Meyer's mind about me and my play. He began to substitute for me in certain situations. My regular playing time decreased toward the end of the year. I wound up playing more on special teams. Whatever was going on, I would soon learn. But I still did my best.

It was as a special teams member that I scored my first offensive touchdown in the pros. The circumstances could not have been better. The Colts were visiting Miami, playing in Joe Robbie Stadium. My parents and some of my friends were in the stands. My mom still likes to tell the story.

The Colts offense had a drive stall deep in Dolphins' territory. We had to go for the field goal. I was the wing on the field goal team—the person who lines up at the end of the line, in the backfield, and forces all oncoming rushers to the outside of the ball's path.

Nothing was unusual about the play until the ball was snapped. It was high and hard. Our holder went up to get it, but it bounced through his hands . . . and into the hands of our kicker.

"Fire, Fire!" the holder yelled, as Mike Wood, our kicker began to experience his own Garo Yepremian moment (Garo was a Miami Dolphins kicker in the early Dolphin dynasty years who is famous for botching this same type of play on a field goal try in the Super Bowl, no less).

My parents, sitting on about the three yard line, could hear our team yelling "fire" (meaning a fumble or mishandling of the ball). When they heard that call, certain people were programmed to break out of formation and into a specified pass route.

Poor Mike, his eyes filled with terror, headed to his right, as did the entire Dolphin defense. No one on that side was open, so he turned and floated one across the field to me.

I thought it would never get to me. It eventually did, and I waltzed into the end zone as the Dolphin home crowd fell silent.

Mom has talked a lot about that play since then. She was very proud of my touchdown.

Although I never asked Coach Shula about it, it could have been another "Barry Krauss moment" like my earlier Notre Dame moment. (Details to follow.)

Even though I was uncertain of my future with the Colts, I was happy we had a good year, posting a 9-7 record. We also made the playoffs. It was an unusual situation. Our last game of the year was with the Cleveland Browns. Our playoff game the next week was also with the Cleveland Browns. We beat them to end the season. They beat us in the playoffs the next week.

It was in that second Cleveland game that I took the hardest lick I ever took in football.

It was late in the game, and we were down. Bernie Kosar was moving his offense, killing us and the clock at the same time. We had to make something happen, so we called a blitz.

Remember, I was in the best shape of my life, as fast and as big as I had ever been. As my hole opened I was already going full speed. Little Ernest Byner, a running back from East Carolina, stepped up in the hole. Ernest was coiled so tightly he was shaking, and all the while his legs were pumping ninety-to-nothing.

At this point I saw my options as pretty simple: do a swim move to get by him, or run over him. Since Kosar was killing us and running over Byner would be quicker, I opted to take that route.

Ladies and gentlemen, I am barely alive today to tell you this story. At 5'11" and two hundred pounds, Ernest Byner packed one hell of a punch. It was like hitting a wall—a concrete-and-steel-reinforced wall. I lost every filling in my mouth.

Needless to say, I didn't get to Bernie Kosar. I'm not even sure I got to the sideline by myself.

I had no idea that game would be the last for me in a Colts uniform.

Ten years later, at a charity golf tournament, I got a chance to talk to Ernest again.

"Do you remember that hit in Cleveland?" I asked.

A huge smile broke over his face. "Man, that was my best ever!"

15

It's Easy—Just Take a Right in Cleveland and Keep Driving

At the end of the 1988 season my contract was coming up for renewal. I approached Ron Meyer and asked what his plans were for me the following year. His plan was to let me go as a Plan B free agent. He told me I should take any offer I could get.

At the time there was a difference between free agency and Plan B free agency. NFL teams could choose the thirty-seven free agent players they wanted to protect and allow all other players to become Plan B free agents. If one of those thirty-seven protected free agents made a deal, the acquiring team had to compensate the former team, usually with a draft choice.

The Plan B free agents were free to talk to and take offers from any team in the league. If the player signed with a new team, that team owed nothing to his former team. If the player wound up re-signing with his original team, he would automatically get a 10 percent raise.

Plan B free agency later became the grounds for bidding wars, and tremendous problems arose for the NFL, the owners, and the players' association.

Basically, letting me go as a Plan B player was Meyer's way of cutting me, getting rid of me in the least offensive way possible.

I had already been approached by Ernie Accorsi, the former Colts general manager, who was now with the Cleveland Browns. Ernie had recruited Bud Carson as the defensive coordinator. Bud was the man behind the "Steel Curtain" defense all of those years at Pittsburgh. He knew me as a player and knew I could run his defense.

They got together and made me a deal. I would be a Cleveland Brown in 1989.

Darcy and I had only recently had our first child, a little girl we named Charlsie, so we decided that I would go on to Cleveland and take care of the details of getting a place to live before they would move over. That way she had plenty of time to recuperate.

I went over, found an apartment, and began to work out prior to training camp.

The Browns were a good team. The previous year they had beaten us in the playoffs. One of the things that made them good was their veteran defense—Hanford Dixon, Bubba Baker, and a group of other talented players. When some of the players found out the Browns had acquired me—and why—they were not happy. Bud Carson wanted me to head their defensive team because I knew all of his schemes and could quickly teach the other guys. Therefore, before I even stepped on the field I felt a little uncomfortable.

Not a deterrent for one Barry Krauss. I would have to work really hard to again earn the respect of my teammates and coaches. I had done it before. I could do it again.

When I arrived in Cleveland, I was already tired. At camp I started overdoing my physical training. It was the same in practice. Most important, I didn't listen to my body.

Within several weeks I had both knees so swollen and painful I couldn't play on them. And when I did play, it wasn't good.

Darcy and Charlsie made the move to Cleveland several weeks into camp. As soon as Darcy really got settled in, Bud called me in for "the talk."

He had to cut me, he said.

I was really down emotionally. I came home that day and told Darcy, "I'm done. I'm out of football."

"What will we do?" she asked.

"Go back to Indy," I responded without a clue. It was all I could think of. We'd been happy there.

The following day we loaded a U-Haul and started driving back to Indy. That drive was, without a doubt, the most depressing time I have ever spent in a car. I had just been forcibly removed from the game I dearly loved. I was already entering the early stages of separation anxiety, a very common malady that befalls football players at all levels when the game is finally over for them. To top it off, as I was driving the U-Haul, Darcy would pull up beside me and point to our baby in her car seat—Charlsie was obviously bawling for all she was worth. It was a high-stress time.

The day after we got back to Indianapolis I was outside unloading the truck when Darcy came outside with the phone.

"Somebody wants to talk to you."

"I don't want to talk to anybody, honey," I said, totally dejected and feeling sorry for myself.

"You might want to take this one," she said smiling. "It's Don Shula."

My first thought was that this had to be a joke. Sure, one of my so-called friends was pulling a scam on me.

I took the phone. "Hello?"

"Hey, Barry, this is Don Shula."

"Yeah, right, Don!"

"Well, I just wanted to find out if you still want to play some football."

"Sure," I said in an obviously sarcastic tone.

"Let me get someone else to talk with you," said the voice on the other end of the line.

"Barry," a familiar voice boomed, "it's George Hill."

"Is this for real, George?" I responded, trying not to sound too stupid.

"Yeah! Shula wants you. Offerdahl is holding out, and so is another guy. He wants you!"

"Wow!" was the best response I could come up with at the moment. "Great! Let me work out some details, and I'll call you back."

At that moment my biggest concern was how Darcy would take another move, this time to Miami. With a new baby, Miami, at least half a world away from Indy and her parents, might be a challenge. Particularly since she had never liked Cleveland.

Some history is pertinent here. When I had signed with the Browns, the first thing she asked was, "What are their team colors?"

"Orange and brown," I responded.

"Ummm," was her lackluster reply. "What emblem is on their helmets?" she followed up, obviously giving the city and the team a second chance.

"They don't have one," I said, as I swallowed hard.

Darcy didn't dig Cleveland from the start.

Now, after packing up and driving back to Indy from Cleveland—with a screaming baby in the car for most of the way—here it was happening again.

"What color are the Dolphins?" she asked.

"Orange and turquoise."

She smiled just a little.

"That's nice. What do they have on their helmets?" she continued.

"A dolphin."

"Way cool!" she said, now beaming. "Great. We can go."

I love this woman!

Of course, this was also my dream come true.

In preparation for my first Dolphin game in Miami, I called all of my old high school buddies and told them to get down there. I'll never forget having on that Dolphin uniform for the first time in Joe Robbie Stadium. As I was warming up, I heard those old friends yelling from the stands.

I was living the dream.

However, the dream also had a few bumps in the road.

I had what I felt was a good camp leading into the opening game. Yet Don Shula used me only sparingly in the first three games. I would play on special teams mostly, sometimes in special situations.

After the third week of limited duty, I approached Coach Shula.

"I know you didn't bring me here to be a special teams man," I said. "I'm an eleven-year veteran."

"That's the problem," he responded quickly. "You walk around here, and even in practice, like an old veteran with nothing better to do."

From that day on I was always going wide open.

The next week—as luck would have it—we played Cleveland. I caught Eric Metcalf on the sideline and threw him into Bud Carson, who had cut me only a month earlier.

"Who the hell cut him?" I heard him chuckling—for my sake I am sure—as I was heading back onto the field.

The very next week we played the Indianapolis Colts and beat them soundly. Although I didn't have the chance to throw a full-grown person at him, I hoped Ron Meyer was thinking the same thing.

Those two victories were part of the Miami Dolphins six-game winning streak that year. The team played great all year up until the Pittsburgh game close to the end of the season. In Miami that game is almost as legendary as the Noah's Ark story in the Bible.

We were up 14–0 over the Steelers early. At around half-time the heavens opened up, and it rained buckets. Joe Robbie Stadium was awash—literally. Waterfalls were spilling down the aisles and over the seats. The rain kept coming . . . and so did the Steelers.

For some reason they thrived on it. And they wound up beating us.

We were not the same team after that. That loss took the wind completely out of our sails.

It was a wonderful year though. It was even more wonderful to be back in

Florida, close to Mom and Dad. They got to come to a lot of my games in Miami. It was wonderful to be around them again.

At the end of my first year with the Dolphins, I was named the defensive player of the year for the team. I was, and still am, very proud of that. I was a new player on a veteran defense, a newcomer whom Don Shula had put his trust in, and I had delivered.

It truly was a great year.

Don't get me wrong, I also had some "Barry Krauss" moments with the Dolphins. One of these is among my all-time most embarrassing moments.

I realize that everyone has embarrassing moments. No matter how many people are involved, those moments are always a humbling experience. Yet, have one of those on national television in front of ten million people and you have really come to know embarrassment.

The place was again Miami's Joe Robbie Stadium, the following year, 1989. We were playing the Green Bay Packers in the third game of the season; we had already beaten the Browns and the Colts in our first two outings. I was still trying to prove to Don Shula that he had made the right move in bringing me to the Dolphins. Playing for Coach Shula was like playing for Coach Bryant—you always wanted to prove your worth.

Green Bay ran the ball to the sideline and I pursued strong. This is where everything gets a little fuzzy. As we all closed on the sideline something happened to me: I still don't know if I was bumped, clipped, pushed from behind, or what. I flew across the sideline, over the pile and directly into the ground.

The first thing I noticed was that the left side of my face was numb: I tried to feel it with my hand. At that point I noticed that I was bleeding.

Luckily, there was an injury time-out called because I was on the Packers' sideline.

"He didn't even hit anyone," I heard some unidentified Packer say through his chuckle.

By this time I was struggling to my feet . . . dazed, bloody, and with a huge chunk of sod in my facemask.

"Pretty inspirational," I thought, not realizing I was still dazed.

I ran back onto the field and into the huddle.

"Come on guys, we can do it!" I yelled authoritatively.

No one responded. Blank looks all around.

"We can!" I barked again. "Come on, fellas!"

Still no response. Finally, I heard an unfamiliar voice.

"Man, Dude, you're in the wrong huddle."

During my third and last year with the Dolphins, my knees were killing me. Yet I did everything I could to conceal how bad they were. But my play was suffering, and my teammates knew they weren't getting the "real Barry Krauss."

George Hill called me at home and told me the bad news. He was very nice and very understanding.

"I have to cut you," he said, apologetically.

This time I knew it was over. I was so dejected that I didn't even want to go in and clean out my locker.

Later that week Darcy tried to talk me into going in to get my stuff at the practice camp.

I was too embarrassed. I just didn't want to see any of them again.

About a week later, we were out for a drive. It was something we would do just to pass the time. When Darcy made this particular turn, her motive became clear. She pulled into the college where the Dolphins were working out. She was taking me to get things, my mementos of a life of professional football.

As soon as I walked in, the whole coaching staff was there. Everyone was wonderful. Coach Shula took me aside.

"Thanks for playing for me," he said as he hugged me.

Playing football was over for Barry Krauss.

This was the storybook ending. It was OK to let go now.

I could be normal now. I could have a life. I could spend time with my wife and family.

But football remained, as everyone knew it would, still a huge part of my life. I couldn't bring myself to leave it altogether. I agreed to do color commentary for the local Colts television broadcasts. I also did a Colts radio show for a number of years and called the play-by-play on radio broadcasts of high school football games.

I became involved with a Minor League football team, the Indiana Tornados, and later became its coach and owner.

With all of this football, one might think I did not really have much time with Darcy. We did have some time together. Our youngest daughter, Savannah, was born in 1994, and Karsten, her little brother, was born in April of 1998.

Karsten, Charlsie and Savannah know how to manipulate their dad. (From the author's collection)

Yet I have always stayed close to football. Football people are my type of people.

And being away from the game, I realized just how much respect I had for the really great men I had been honored to play for, Paul W. Bryant and Don Shula.

Fifteen years after I retired, I played in the Jimmy Rane Golf Tournament in Auburn, Alabama, and Coach Shula was the guest speaker. Knowing he would be there, I took my old Dolphins helmet, jersey, and a team picture for him to autograph. This was the first time I had a real opportunity to tell him how much I loved him and respected him. We sat in his room talking about football, Coach Bryant, and life for an hour and a half.

Before I left, I told him thank you—not just for the autographs—but for everything.

16

My Longest Love Affair

Playing football at the University of Alabama under Paul W. Bryant was a very significant part of my life. Playing on a national championship team gave me a rare and important experience in the development of my character and personal life. Being the central figure in "The Goal Line Stand" opened the door to opportunities that, up to that point, I had thought were impossible to achieve.

The 1979 Sugar Bowl was a wonderful moment in college football. It was one of the rarest moments in bowl history prior to the BCS, when the number-one and number-two teams had the opportunity of actually deciding the national championship on the football field.

Alabama players and fans, in particular, appreciated that fact. The previous year, a number-five Notre Dame team had vaulted over three other teams, including Alabama coming off a bowl win, to be handed a mythical, but still recognized, championship.

The 1979 Sugar Bowl, it seemed, was blessed in that all bodies of the universe had aligned perfectly to give the University of Alabama this opportunity.

What makes the moment special even today is quite simple—it means so much to the people it affected—*the fans.*

The fans make football special.

Alabama fans have stories of how the fourth-down play changed them, or changed Alabama football from a runner-up throughout the decade of the 1970s, to the national champion.

I love talking to the fans. I love hearing how much Alabama and that play mean to them.

Their stories interest me as much as my story interests them. And if talking to me about that event—twenty-five or thirty years down the road—helps them rekindle and relive that moment, I welcome that opportunity. After all, the event was ours, not mine.

And they have made my involvement in this team very memorable.

I am constantly reminded of the blessings, and responsibilities, of my love affair with Alabama fans.

On September 1, 2001, I served as honorary captain for the season-opening, nationally televised game with UCLA. My only job, it seemed, was to run the ball onto the field and give it to the officials. I was flattered to be asked and even happier when I learned that I could share this wonderful experience with my wife, Darcy.

Now, Darcy is a true Indiana girl. She had heard that there is a game in the South just as big as basketball is in Indiana, but she wasn't convinced.

On that Saturday Darcy stood on the fifty yard line, mouth agape, as eighty-six thousand screaming fans watched the screen above the south end zone of the stadium for the highlights from the 1976 Liberty Bowl against UCLA, where I intercepted a pass and ran it in. It got even louder when the footage of the ultimate play of The Goal Line Stand popped up.

As I was introduced and ran the game ball on the field, the stands erupted. I was emotionally overwhelmed. At the end of a three-minute standing ovation, with more than a few tears welling in my eyes, I trotted off the field to see Darcy, mouth still agape, staring at me as if she were trying to see someone else deep inside who all these people were so crazy about.

"Wow," she managed to verbalize through tears. "This is cool."

It was. It is.

Thank you, Alabama fans, for making another wonderful moment.

17

The Journey

My third-grade teacher, Ms. Sayer, was a wonderful lady. As I said earlier, I was somewhat rambunctious as a child (and all the rest of my life, up until this moment) and often found myself at odds with teachers and their rules. Ms. Sayer was different. She appreciated me. She allowed me to be me, with some necessary guidance, of course.

More important, she inspired me. She talked to me. She treated me like a person.

Shortly after I was picked up by the Miami Dolphins, Ms. Sayer sent me a handwritten congratulatory note. In it she talked about being my teacher in the third grade and how I had told her that my goal, my dream, was to play football for Coach Don Shula and the Miami Dolphins. Quite honestly, even though I do remember dreaming that dream, I never realized I had shared it with an adult, particularly a teacher.

She went on to talk about how I had done something that millions of people all around the world so desperately wanted to do—live out a childhood dream.

Of course, she was right.

I called and made arrangements to go back to see her—she was still teaching—and tell her students about how dreams really do come true.

Yet, retrospectively, I realized that living that dream, accomplishing that goal, was not the most important thing in my life.

What was most important to me—then as a Miami Dolphin and today as a retired football player, full-time husband, and proud father—was the journey. That journey—from the third grade, through the angst of growing up, to the guidance of Coach Bryant, to that Chance of a Lifetime in the Sugar Bowl, to becoming a first-round draft choice and playing twelve years of professional football and retiring from the Miami Dolphins—was more important than the dream itself.

Yes, life is the journey, not the destination.

This is a lesson taught poignantly by Danny Hulse, a brave young boy from Anderson, Indiana, where the Colts held camp each year.

Danny was a big Colts fan. I first met him in 1984, the club's inaugural year in

Indianapolis. He and his parents, John and Nancy Hulse, lived just around the corner from our practice facility. As a two-year-old child he was diagnosed with a rare circulatory disease, which basically destroyed his legs—both had to be amputated. Danny would roll his wheelchair up close to the field so he could see everything. He also loved to get every autograph he could.

During that first camp, I got with Johnny Scott, our equipment man, and we gave Danny a Colts jersey with his name on it, along with the number 1. (I felt he was our number-one fan.) Nancy and John were grateful because Danny lived for the Colts . . . literally. He wore his jersey everywhere.

The next year Danny was there again. This time he was bald. When I finally got to talk to Nancy, I learned that he had been diagnosed with brain cancer. He had lost his hair from the chemotherapy. The next day I brought a huge umbrella for Danny's wheelchair. He and I became very close; "my buddy," I always called him. I gave Danny every kind of Colts memorabilia: footballs, sweatshirts, even one of my game jerseys.

The next year at camp, I learned that Danny had been diagnosed with lung cancer. It had taken its toll on the little boy by the time I saw him. Of course, it had also been rough on John and Nancy.

One day I received a call from Danny. He asked that I come to see him in the hospital. I went that day right after practice. Nancy told me he had already stopped breathing twice since he was admitted.

When I got in to see him, his bloated and swollen face couldn't hide his beaming smile. He handed me a charm that had been engraved: "To Barry, Love Danny." After we acted up and played a while, I had the opportunity to pull Nancy aside and ask, "Why did he do that?"

"Barry, he wants to let the people he loves know that he is getting his affairs in order," she said without hesitation.

In the off-season of 1988, as I was in Cleveland getting ready for camp, I heard Danny was again in the hospital. I called him and told him I was going to try to get back to see him.

"No, you don't need to come," he said. "God's not ready for me yet."

Nancy Hulse called me a couple of days later to tell me that Danny had died.

"I'm on my way," I responded.

"No," she was adamant. "Don't come. He was facing death when he met you. You extended his life for at least two years. He would want you to remember him the way he was, alive."

Several days later I was talking to one of the Colts equipment men, also Danny's friend, who had been to the funeral. He told me, "He was holding a Teddy Bear and wearing a Colts jersey."

"Wow, he was wearing that #1 jersey we gave him?"

He was silent for a couple of moments.

"No, Barry, he was wearing *your* jersey."

I didn't know what to say. I still don't. Except, Danny made the best of his journey, and he taught me to try to make the best of mine.

Getting to know Danny over those years was a wonderful experience. We only had a few moments at a time together, spread over several years. However, my relationship with Danny taught me how important the little things in life are in making our lives—our journeys—truly worth living.

Looking back on my journey, I realize I have experienced millions of those little moments, little lessons in my journey, which made my life better. Some were dramatic. Others were simple. More important, these experiences have inspired me, shaped me, marked me, and made me.

Paul Crane, my linebacker coach at Alabama, taught me to love pickled eggs. Every time we got in the car together I knew he would invariably stop at some tiny, out-of-the-way gas station/general store that proudly displayed a huge jar of pickled eggs. He knew where all of the best pickled eggs were throughout the South. Today I have a pickled egg jar on our counter at home.

Tony Nathan laughed at me—howled would be a better description—as he watched me eat ribs one day. I obviously needed serious help. He took me under his wing, made me his personal project, and taught me the right way to eat ribs. We were extremely dedicated—we practiced a lot. I can still smell the wonderful aroma and hear jukebox tunes drifting from Archibald's Barbeque in Northport. You will be happy to know that I can still clean a rib better than an army of ants.

My journey included innumerable trips to see half a movie. Coach Bryant would always take the team to a theater the night before a game in order to keep us from getting caught up in the revelry. We would sit down, get into it, then somewhere right around the second plot point, he would come in and announce it was time to go. I love seeing the endings today on the cable channels. Who says there's nothing good on TV?

My journey featured my mother and father's unrelenting love, for which I am eternally grateful.

My journey included steaks on game day and hot dogs with cheese during the week when I graded lower than 70 percent.

It also included the impossible. After sitting by Mary Harmon Bryant at a pregame meal and complaining mildly about the dress code for players who were not dressing out for the game, Mrs. Bryant took it up with Coach. The next week we no longer had to wear the houndstooth blazers to the game.

Bruce Bolton and I learned that playing on special teams can get you to the varsity quicker than talent. I got my number 77 by being a tackle on the punting team.

I learned that the Alabama family was real. I have always relished the times we can get together. Joe Namath even made time to call my mom when I was hurt, giving her words of encouragement and support.

I learned that riding the team bus with a police escort is the absolute best way to travel.

On my journey I learned that flying in a big jet home with my family for Christmas—after having a great game, beating UCLA, and being named MVP of the Liberty Bowl in Memphis—was much better than climbing back on one of those two wildly smoking, twin-engine planes for the return to Tuscaloosa.

My journey also included learning how to deer hunt with some of my teammates from the country. Of course, I did it the Barry Krauss way. After a big country breakfast at four in the morning I would get in my deer stand and sleep the morning away. I never saw a deer of any type. If one came by, I probably scared it with my snoring. I loved the experience. It was wonderful. I would do it all again some cold morning next January.

My journey included learning the ancient time-honored method of curing injuries, taught by the famous University of Alabama health guru and head trainer Jim Goostree.

"Put some iiice on it!" he would say about any injury from turf toe to a migraine headache. Goose also spread the word about biology, particularly at those gut checks in practice. "You know," he said philosophically, "the body is a wonderful thing. You will always pass out before you die."

My journey included a gazillion hours of training in the lower gym in the coliseum.

Even worse, I spent several lifetimes in the zoot-suit—the closest point to hell on the face of the earth. The zoot-suit was a heavily padded suit—think of a catcher's chest protector in baseball—that covered your entire body. We would have to put this unwieldy thing on—ten or fifteen pounds of hot padding—and take on the running backs as they tried to cut us, block us, or just run over us. These times were my personal "gut checks." After thirty minutes or so, my suit would be soaked with sweat—now making it closer to twenty-five pounds. Inside the contraption the temperature was probably substantially above the 130 degrees it was on the Thomas Field artificial turf.

I would try to take my mind off how miserable I was by glancing around the treetops and building roofs, hoping a sniper would put me out of my misery. I wanted to die because I couldn't quit.

I learned that everything you do in life can have an impact broader than you ever expected—positively or negatively. Cornelius Bennett, the five-time All-Pro linebacker, once said that my picture on the *Sports Illustrated* cover, hitting Guman on the fourth-down play of The Goal Line Stand, was what made him decide to go to Alabama. That was perhaps the greatest thing anyone has ever said about me.

I laughed when I learned the wonderful story that came out of Ken Donahue's funeral in March 2001. Coach Donahue would have loved the fact that he was a part of it. It seems that a small boy noticed the huge ring on the hand of Tennessee Coach Phillip Fulmer and asked what it was.

"That's the 1998 national championship ring, young man," Fulmer responded proudly.

The little boy looked to the man standing just a step away from Fulmer and asked him the same question.

"Well, son," said Clem Gryska, now retired from the Alabama staff, "it *is* a national championship ring. But I'm not sure which one. . . . I have seven of them!"

My beautiful and loving mother taught me that not being rich was not a sin. She was constantly sending care packages to me, which of course we all shared. My Bryant Hall neighbors would have sworn that I lived totally off of tuna fish and sardines.

My quiet and strong-willed father handed down to me some of his athletic prowess and the invaluable traits of integrity and patience.

I learned that that skinny blond-headed guy who came to our pregame breakfasts and sat by Coach Bryant was Jerry Pate, and he had won some big pro golf tournament as an amateur. Today after thirty years of playing golf, I revel in having been in the same room with the man.

I realized as a player that the folks who come to games in motor homes are the smartest football fans on the planet. And, if they're Alabama fans, they are the nicest.

Adding it all up, I have learned that I am among the luckiest people in the world—to have had my life, my journey.